Spirit
Eyes

Spirit
Eyes

Jennifer Mackenzie

WESTBOW
PRESS®
A DIVISION OF THOMAS NELSON
& ZONDERVAN

WestBow Press books may be ordered through booksellers or by contacting:

WestBow Press
A Division of Thomas Nelson & Zondervan
1663 Liberty Drive
Bloomington, IN 47403
www.westbowpress.com
844-714-3454

Because of the dynamic nature of the Internet, any web addresses or links contained in this book may have changed since publication and may no longer be valid. The views expressed in this work are solely those of the author and do not necessarily reflect the views of the publisher, and the publisher hereby disclaims any responsibility for them.

Any people depicted in stock imagery provided by Getty Images are models, and such images are being used for illustrative purposes only. Certain stock imagery © Getty Images.

Scripture taken from the King James Version of the Bible.

Scripture quotations taken from The Holy Bible, New International Version® NIV® Copyright © 1973 1978 1984 2011 by Biblica, Inc. TM. Used by permission. All rights reserved worldwide.

Scripture quotations marked TPT are from The Passion Translation®. Copyright © 2017, 2018 by Passion & Fire Ministries, Inc. Used by permission. All rights reserved. ThePassionTranslation.com.

ISBN: 978-1-6642-0606-9 (sc)
ISBN: 978-1-6642-0607-6 (e)

Print information available on the last page.

WestBow Press rev. date: 01/18/2021

Dedication

My sincere and abundant gratitude goes out first to The Holy Spirit, the One who continues to prompt, teach and direct me. I'm so honored He wanted me to share His stories.

I would like to dedicate this book to my 3 beautiful children, and 10 grandchildren. So many of these stories would not exist without you. You are my joy and great rewards. I love you all dearly!

And to my treasured friends who believed in me and encouraged me to press on to finish this book. I could not have stayed on task without your uplifting words. Thank you for believing in me and pushing me to get the job done. My heart is full because of friends like you. And lastly, a special thanks to Susan McBride for her artwork for the cover and my Editor, Melissa A Creel. Much love and thanks to you all.

Being confident of this very thing, that He which has begun a good work in you will perform it until the day of Jesus Christ. (Philippians 1:6, NIV)

Contents

Introduction

When I first heard God speak to me, I couldn't believe my ears. It's true. I was stunned and bewildered. I asked myself, am I really hearing from God? I soon responded to what I had heard and a miracle happened. Then He spoke a second time, then a third and fourth and so on. Can you fathom God speaking? The fact is this: God communicates to us all of the time. We just need to tune into the Spirit and listen.

What you think if I told would you that I have witnessed actual angels and demons in action? Society thinks of the supernatural as something mystical, but for God it is natural. Many of us have read of all the mighty works accomplished by God's chosen men and women of the Bible and we stand in amazement. The truth is, we too can walk in the supernatural things of God just as they did. Some of us actually do, every day. I can honestly say that, because I am one of them. By God's grace, I have witnessed and participated in many miracles throughout my lifetime. Did you know that the Bible has 66 books written by 40 different writers over a span of several thousand years? And the words written confirm one another, all inspired by God! If you ask me, I believe that God's story continues even today through the life of every believing Christian. We are the New Testament.

It's my hope that the supernatural stories that you read will help build your faith and encourage you to receive The Holy Spirit, who opens your eyes to the spiritual realm. My prayer is that you come into a closer walk with our precious Lord and Savior, Jesus Christ. If you so desire, you can become full of His presence and experience the richness that only He can bring.

Living life from a spiritual standpoint is very thrilling and exciting. In addition to that, the spiritual life is also filled with pain and suffering, because it is tied to the physical realm. Therefore, we all experience that. When tragedy hit my home, I realized we were truly in a war!

With the most excruciating experience of losing my daughter Katherine, and granddaughter Diane 12 years later. I took notice on how real the devil is. I have realized that we are at war with an unseen enemy seeking to capture our soul. Our enemy has a name. His name is Satan. Are you *equipped and ready* to win your war against him? It's a must for us to be prepared. One thing I know is that the enemy is **not** playing and neither should we.

Chapter

1

Write the Book!

Time is short and so much is to be said. I want to obey what I feel God instructing me to do.

"Write the book!" she said firmly *during a real estate continuing education class.*

What! I said to myself. *The instructor just spoke to me through the Spirit of God.* I couldn't believe what I just heard, nor could I get my mind back on the subject being taught. It was supernatural and I knew it! The instructor and I had never met on a personal level. We knew nothing about each other. I only knew her as a woman who was competent in real estate.

I already had all the necessary credits for my real estate business, yet I kept being prompted to attend this particular class via my email. I felt as though this information was popping up in my email for a reason, a particular knowing by the Spirit of God. I had no idea why, but at that time in my life, I had already become familiar with God's nudges well enough to know when I should respond to the promptings.

So, in following God's lead, I went to the class. My vocation was in real estate, but my true passion was sharing Jesus so that others could find the same peace that I feel within, because of Him. During the middle of the session on "Know Your Niche Market," the instructor Cynthia started walking directly towards me while talking about the subject. She then stopped and looked directly at me. Unexpectedly she said, *"Write the book!"*

I was stunned. I looked around to see if she was speaking to someone else. But no! She couldn't have. I was the only one sitting at the table. And to top it off, no one was behind me. I'm not even sure she realized that she said it. She didn't skip a beat, but continued her lecture on "Knowing Your Niche Market." I couldn't get her outburst off my mind. So, after the class, I asked her if I could speak with her for a few minutes. Cynthia responded, "Of course, follow me to my office."

Cynthia was a very influential and intelligent lady. As I had mentioned, we had not known each other on a personal level apart from seeing one another in class and occasionally passing in the hallway. As we entered her office she asked, "So, how can I help?"

My first reply unfortunately wasn't the one I really wanted to mention. The reply I settled with was, "Well, I would like to find my Niche Market." With a raise of her brow she asked, "What market of people are you trying to reach?"

With that question in mind, my first thought was *all people.* Cynthia noticed my blank expression. "What is your passion?" she prompted. Her many questions, good questions at that, caused me to think. It was then that I spoke what was really on my heart, "My passion has nothing to do with real estate, it's sharing the Gospel and seeing *people restored back to God.*" Cynthia listened to my every word. "My desire is to share Jesus with everyone. It's in my heart to get as many people saved that I can. My desire has *nothing* to do with my real estate profession."

At this declaration, my instructor sat down. She placed her hands over each knee and leaned forward. The way she leaned forward, in my opinion, was a sign of authority. Looking directly at me, she said in a convincing manner, **"Write the book!"**

Tears welled up in my eyes at her command. I got choked up feeling like I was going to cry. "What did you say?" I asked as she repeated herself.

"Write the book!" She said.

"But I need to work and earn an income," I told her holding back my emotion. "I'm the sole supporter of my household."

"Just do what He says and write the book!" Cynthia made clear. "He's going to roll out the red carpet. Trust Him."

My instructor knew absolutely nothing about me. I was just another student that attended her continuing education classes. But I knew right then she was speaking on behalf of The Holy Spirit. I know God's voice, and that was without a doubt Him speaking through her! I felt the need to be obedient to what God was calling me to do. I believe that many would be blessed, myself especially! I learned that whenever God is involved in something, you should just go with it, even if it doesn't make sense. Once I left her office, I went home to begin. But, first, let me catch you up on a few important things.

It has been quite a journey since I surrendered my life to Jesus. Right away, I was shown a multitude of unexplainable things. Heavenly things became very real to me. God, in all His glory, allowed me to see angelic beings when I was only 24-years-old. Since my first sighting of the angels, I have witnessed others. And not just angels but demons too. With *spirit eyes,* I have been used directly and indirectly for miracles which seemed impossible to explain.

In 2011, the spirit of God impressed on my heart to write a book. At first, I did not act on this thought, but simply kept it in the back of my mind, telling myself that maybe *someday* or *one day* I would write. I continued to wrestle with the idea of starting a book. That when I understood that it was indeed the spirit of God directing me. I knew the instructor was not to be ignored, her inexplicable comments made my decision easy.

Another valuable thing to know is this: I **dream** a lot. I mean like − *a lot.* I try to journal my dreams as soon as I receive them because I know that God speaks to me in my dreams. He speaks in your dreams too. It's one of the many ways He communicates to us. Many times, God uses our dreams as warnings. He has saved me from making bad decisions that could have easily turned into disasters. Some dreams instruct us for the good of others and even the nation.

There are times when I see images or words. God has even made His communication techniques to be very simple and childlike; a very obvious indication of what He is revealing. I don't always understand every dream, but at the right moment, I receive revelations through events occurring that connect the dots back to my dream. Over time, I have learned to not be afraid of what is being seen in my dreams, although at times I do get scared. If I don't remember or understand a dream, I can rest with peace knowing that the Lord will seal the instruction of it at the right moment.

For God does speak-now one way, now another-though no one perceives it. In a dream, in a vision of the night, when deep sleep falls on people as they slumber in their beds, he may speak in their ears and terrify them with warnings, to turn them from wrongdoing and keep them from pride, to preserve them from the pit, their lives from perishing by the sword. (Job 33:14-18)

Journaling is another way that God communicates with me. As I write, it brings me a sense of order as I put my thoughts on paper. I find this method to be therapeutic, but most importantly a very personal time with God. When I journal, my writing turns into a conversation with God. He joins me and we express our thoughts with one another. Quite often I receive answers to my questions from Him.

If you don't think God is speaking, try it out for yourself. I feel a much closer and connected to God through my journaling. Putting my thoughts on paper makes me aware of where I am in my walk with Him. He causes me to make corrections to bad behaviors or wrong beliefs. His encouragement and instructions are always lined up perfectly with His Word in the Scriptures. His responses to my questions always bring me clarity and peace. Most of the time He answers my questions with a question. This always causes me to see the answer.

As mentioned, the same day the Lord spoke through Cynthia, I went home to begin writing the book. I remember looking to God for some inspiration. I didn't know where to begin. I started a conversation with The Holy Spirit about what to write, but I began to feel overwhelmed. I knew nothing about writing, let alone writing something for others to read. I knew this whole book thing was God's plan and not mine, so I found myself putting my trust in Him from the beginning and doing what He said.

While praying, God reminded me of all the journal entries I had made over the years. One particular composition book was highlighted in my spirit's eye. When I picked up the journal, it literally opened to a page with two dreams which I had recorded some time back. Coincidence? No way!

I had written one dream on top of an older dream. In the first dream, I saw the Father coming down the stairs with a stack of books in His hands, bringing them to me. The second dream was written in the dark. I had grabbed the journal while half asleep, barely sitting up when I recorded two words. I happened to record the two words over the stairwell dream. Of course, I hadn't meant to do that, but God did. I wrote, **Expressive Writings.**

He was showing me that my writing was to be shared so that it would bring many people the awareness of their feelings, as well as mine. He made the task of writing much easier. God said in His Word, "My yoke is easy and my burden light," so I had no reason to carry around such weight. I just needed to express myself by conveying my thoughts and feelings on paper. That very night He confirmed what I was to do with another dream!

I saw two pencils, golden-amber in color and they were floating in the air. The number two represented witness or testimony, while the golden-amber color represented God's Glory and anointing. This was God informing me that this book and the many books to follow were the testimonies He has given me. To this day, I still see things in the supernatural almost daily. Seeing people being healed and delivered from physical or emotional issues is a normal thing for me. By no means do I live a so-called "normal life," but I enjoy walking in the spirit. I **don't** want the norm! My life is way more exciting walking and living by the supernatural. Writing this book of mine is no different.

Chapter

2

Real or Imagination

The spiritual world, it real or is it just our imagination? Do you remember hearing stories about the devil? Did you ever believe those stories? When I was younger, I thought all the devil stories I had heard were fabricated like dark children's stories. I had the picture painted in my mind of the devil in the red-hooded-suit holding a pitch fork with horns on his head. No way did I believe that there was a real devil. And that is exactly what the real devil wants everyone to believe!

Satan (the devil) wants you and me to think he's just a cartoon character.

When I turned my heart over to God, I began to **see** much differently, the veil was removed from my eyes. Before it was lifted, I had cried out to God in desperation about whether or not the devil was real. Well, let me tell you, **I got my answer in the most unlikely way!**

As a new believer I was just starting to get to know Jesus. My life had been changing so rapidly, like a whirling funnel cloud. I had more peace on the inside than I ever had before, but things on the outside of me were moving so quickly. I had fallen in love with Jesus and couldn't get enough of His presence. It was as if my eyes were being opened for the very first time. The supernatural (seeing in the spirit) was becoming part of my natural everyday life.

There were exciting and miraculous things happening all around me. The Holy Spirit (who is God inside of me) was revealing Himself to me like never before. I was being made aware of His love and His inward presence daily which I wanted more of. He was teaching me and correcting me on things that I never knew were even real. The best part, was feeling His Perfect love and power which is heart-warming and eye-opening!

An individual doesn't know what they are missing until they've tasted true love that only can come from God above. No one on earth had ever made me feel the love that I was receiving from Jesus. No one.

One of the biggest things that Jesus had taught me was that **the enemy of our soul had been hiding behind the lie of not being real.** That alone was a major part of his deception which kept me and countless others from knowing the truth. Nevertheless, I began to learn very quickly how real the devil was. One of the enemy's main strategies is to **divide families**. If he gets between husband and wife, he destroys the unity of the family.

Ephesians 6 tells us how we must put on the Armor of God to stand against the enemy and overcome his fiery darts.

Finally, be strong in the Lord and in his mighty power. [11] Put on the full armor of God, so that you can take your stand against the devil's schemes. [12] For our struggle is not against flesh and blood, but against the rulers, against the authorities, against the powers of this dark world and against the spiritual forces of evil in the heavenly realms. [13] Therefore put on the full armor of God, so that when the day of evil comes, you may be able to stand your ground, and after you have done everything, to stand. [14] Stand firm then, with the belt of truth buckled around your waist, with the breastplate of righteousness in place, [15] and with your feet fitted with the readiness that comes from the gospel of peace. [16] In addition to all this, take up the shield of faith, with which you can extinguish all the flaming arrows of the evil one. [17] Take the helmet of salvation and the sword of the Spirit, which is the word of God.

¹⁸ And pray in the Spirit on all occasions with all kinds of prayers and requests. With this in mind, be alert and always keep on praying for all the Lord's people. (Eph 6:10-18, NIV)

But the amazing miracles of God were just beginning…

Chapter

3

Born Again

How many churches leave out the fact that the Bible states that we must be born again to enter heaven? **We _must_ be born-again**. In the book of John, Chapter 3, we read that Nicodemus, one of the top religious leaders of his time sneaks out at night to spark a conversation with Jesus. At first, he compliments Him for being such a profound teacher sent from God. Then they got into a whole discussion about being born again. *Jesus answered,*

"Very truly I tell you, no one can enter the kingdom of God unless they are born of water and the Spirit. Flesh gives birth to flesh, but the Spirit [b] gives birth to spirit. You should not be surprised at my saying, 'You [c] must be born again.' The wind blows wherever it pleases. You hear its sound, but you cannot tell where it comes from or where it is going. So, it is with everyone born of the Spirit." [d](John 3: 5-8)

In the natural we are born, but without the Spirit of God living inside of us we are spiritually dead. God is Spirit; and each one of us needs to receive His Spirit within our earthly body. We need The Holy Spirit make us spiritually alive.

Example: When God created man, (Adam) – He breathed inside of him to make him come alive. The Spirit of God becomes alive inside of us but only when He is invited. **Ask, Jesus to breathe His breath in you and come alive!**

God came to us in a bodily form when Mary gave birth to Jesus, the Son of God. Jesus, who literally was born of a virgin, is God in the flesh. God's seed was placed inside of a virgin. Do you get that?! God humbled Himself taking on the form of a man!

Jesus said, "If you've seen me, you've seen the father." The Son is the dazzling radiance of God's splendor. Do you see that? Look at what the Bible says about Jesus who is **"The exact expression of God's true nature—His mirror image!" He holds the universe together and expands it by the mighty power of His spoken word.**

The Gospel of John shows Jesus being both God and The Son of Man. It begins and ends with the assertion that Jesus is God. Jesus is the Lord, the great "I Am" of Exodus 3:14. He is God's Son, who is one with the Father, and boldly He claimed equality with God. But at the same time Jesus is not the same person as the Father, for the Father is greater that He (John 14:28). He took on human flesh, and as a human He became hungry, thirsty and tired. He experienced all human emotions, and when his body was stabbed on the cross, blood and water came out of Him. <u>**Jesus is our divine/human Savior**</u>.

Mankind disobeyed the word of the Lord by listening to the lies of the devil. This cast out devil was on the earth and appeared as a snake in the Garden of Eden, where Adam and Eve resided. Their perfect world was invaded. This devil (snake) convinced Eve that God was not telling them the truth. God has nothing but TRUTH in HIM.

Everything was altered by disobeying God's Word. Starting with Adam and Eve's disobedience or (unbelief)-- this sin grew even more evil. It was most evident with their offspring; we see jealousy, murder, pride, and rebellion, etc. **All evil is the evidence of the wicked lies that you believe.** The wickedness of man became so great that God not only considered putting an end to all-people, but followed through with it! He flooded the earth to destroy the evil that had gotten into the hearts of people.

But, He, being the Merciful God that He is chose to spare mankind instead.

He spared the lives of Noah (because Noah was found to be righteous) and his family, along with two of each kind of animal, a male and female. There was a total of 8 people. Eight being the number of new beginning.

The original plan God had for a perfect world was altered. There was so much sin. Blood needed to be shed to cover it all. But wait! The Father knew this would happen and already had a plan in place to rescue the ones He made in His image. He made a way of escape with His seed. Jesus. The seed of God Himself was placed inside a young, pure hearted virgin woman. God's Son became like you and me with skin and bone. Jesus surrendered His life by shedding His blood to cover the sins of the world! He did this to reconcile us back to the Father. He came to restore what was stolen from us in the beginning.

When you say yes to God, you invite His Living Spirit to reside in your heart, He himself in Spirit form comes and dwells inside of you. He is Spirit and is omnipresent. He doesn't invade your will nor will He come where He is not invited. He draws you to himself prompting you but, waiting for the response to His invite. Think on that!

His very Spirit, the breath (Spirit) of God living inside of the believer! Notice, I said BELIEVER! As I shared, He comes to reside by response to His invitation only. To be born-again, we must allow Him into our heart. Then, and only then can you can develop a personal relationship with Him. God is Spirit and must be worshiped in Spirit and Truth.

Although God's kingdom resides in heaven, He dwells within the body of the believer here on earth. Some people look at the Lord as "The Big God in the Sky." But the truth is to get to know "The Big God in the Sky" you must invite His Spirit into your spirit. After all, you are a spirit inside a body.

When you sense God's spirit hovering over you and knocking on the door of your heart, don't wait, respond! Say YES to Him when He knocks. He's the one that has been searching for you like a lost sheep. He is the good shepherd. Let's stop hiding. The Kingdom of God is at hand, right here and NOW!

Saved Just in Time!

The year was 1968 when I responded to the invite and became born again. I was only 11 years old. I received permission from my Catholic family to attend church with my friend Susan, who lived across the street. Susan and her family were of Baptist background. During the church service, the preacher invited people to come to the altar to receive Christ in their heart. It was the first time I ever heard that I must welcome Jesus in my heart. My church never shared that I needed to invite God in. They only spoke about Jesus, never making Him personal. Instantly, my heart felt drawn to the Pastor's invitation to open myself up to receive Jesus. I responded quickly and headed down to the altar and said a sinner's prayer. Immediately, I felt different, like something had been awoken in me! Something came alive. Nothing dramatic, just different.

I remember crossing the street on my way home from church that day and realizing for the first time the level of my immaturity. I was 11. I never told my parents what I had done in the Baptist church that day but I knew I had undergone a transformation. I was changed.

Life went on as usual, and it wasn't until many years later that my epiphany came. The impact of that particular day was tremendous! For years, I had no clue just how powerful it had been. From that day on, Jesus became part of me, and I can't thank Him enough!

A short time after I had gotten saved (born-again), my grandfather passed away. His death was unexpected. He was only 59 years of age. His lifestyle wasn't always good, yet he had a very soft heart for the things of God and the homeless.

My grandfather started out as a good man. Over the span of

his life he was led astray to better himself financially, in order to provide for his large family of 10. Even though his income wasn't always enough to feed his 8 children, he would still frequently bring strangers home to feed.

To keep up with his debts and bills he began to work for a corrupt company and eventually became a gambler. **He died young because of being led astray working with corrupt company.** There was much controversy about how his death occurred. He drowned and was found only a short distance from his daughter's home.

Was his drowning an accident? My grandfather knew how to swim, was his head struck when he entered the water or did, he receive a blow and then fall into the water? Was it a set-up and he murdered? Did he owe someone money? Maybe the pressures of life had gotten so bad that he decided to take his own life. It is all one big mystery! Or is it?

I learned from Scripture that the sins of the father can be passed down to the 3rd and 4th generation known as a generational curse. But get this - the generational blessings of a Christian continue on for a thousand generations! I thank God for being merciful, because we all need it.

One thing I remember most about my grandfather was how he spoke to me about his need for God. I remember one car ride with him in particular, and he was talking to me about God. I was mesmerized. I had never seen that side of him before. It was during out time together that day that I realized just how special my grandfather was. It was the day that I saw his heart. He did want the goodness of God and wasn't without knowing him.

Life sometimes takes us in a direction of survival. He grew up in an orphanage and he harbored anger from his experiences. But that day, I saw his spiritual side. We tend to carry anger when we don't experience love or how to trust from our childhood.

Here is the reason why I bring up my grandfather's death. I want to share what happened to me shortly after his death. I was 12-years old when my grandfather passed away and the question remained, was his death suicide or something else? Was there a generational curse in my family line that we're dealing with?

Shortly after the time of my grandfather's death, on a day that was no different than any other, the most unusual feeling came over me. I went into the bathroom and for no reason at all I turned on the gas heater without lighting it. I sat down and stayed there to die! What would prompt me to do something so crazy? Suddenly, I stopped and turned the gas OFF! For many years that experience had bothered me and I never spoke about it to anyone. As I got to know Jesus, I asked him what caused me to do that? Why would I do such a thing and try to kill myself? Things weren't perfect in my childhood, but nothing was that bad to have nudged me towards wanting to die. What made me stop? What made me do that in the first place?

It wasn't until 20 years after the incident that I asked Jesus about that dreadful day. And can you believe it? I received the answer! Remember how I had given my heart to Jesus less than a year before my suicidal attempt? Well the Holy Spirit, my comforter, brought me back to that memory and showed me who was behind it all.

I was laying in the presence of God with my eyes closed, **being still** before the Lord. I had asked Him to speak to me …. to reveal what He wanted me to know. A few minutes later, in **a vision** I saw a replay of the near fatal incident from my childhood. However, this time I was able to see the entire scenario and I was shocked to see that *I wasn't alone*. I saw in the spirit realm.

I saw myself go into the bathroom and behind me lurked a tall, dark spirit. He was wearing all black, but I was unable to see his face. This evil spirit (of suicide) was the one driving me into the bathroom and towards the heater to turn on the gas. I then saw a cross separating me and the dark spirit. Standing on the side of me was Jesus with his arm around me. The evil spirit looked as though he had frozen when it saw Jesus! He didn't budge.

Without a word, Jesus sternly looked at this evil spirit as He waved his finger side to side motioning, NO! Then He put His finger to His own chest as though He was saying, "She's mine!" Then the evil spirit quickly backed out of the room.

On that day, Jesus stopped this dark spirit of death from killing me! Because it was right after the death of my grandfather.... was that a familiar spirit in my family line that came? The spirit of suicide.

Thank God, I responded to the spirit drawing me in that little Baptist church that day. I had gotten saved only a short time before this spirit showed up. I honestly don't know what the outcome may have been.

When I say **it's vitally urgent when you feel God drawing you**, I mean it! You must yield to His promptings. You *never* know what evil is lurking around ready to take you out! Without Jesus, I could have died that day. The enemy of our soul is out to steal, kill and destroy us. He will take your life without notice! Without God, we are lost and in grave danger of living without Him in eternity. Forever is a long, long time. I want my eternity with God, not with the enemy of my soul. I want to live with the God of peace and love, not burn and be in torment for all of eternity.

I am so grateful that God kept me from death and destruction. It wasn't until I was 24 that I really got to know Jesus personally. As a young adult I learned about His Spirit and developed an understanding of who He is and what He has done for me. I believe that surrendering to God as a child saved me. I know His plan for me didn't include my life ending in tragedy.

Chapter

4

Angelic Visitation

The year was 1980. Our child was three at the time. We were married only four short years, when my husband and I moved away and left our hometown and everyone close to us. This season was one of the lowest points of my life. I had more pain and discouragement in my heart than I could bear. With feelings of despair and loneliness, on top of rejection, I couldn't take any more heartache.

I had awful thoughts of ending this pain for good. I had no plans of suicide, but many thoughts. I feel that it was a familiar spirit, the same one that visited me that day in the bathroom when I was 12. I hadn't kept close to God during this particular pointe in my life. I actually began questioning so many things about whether God was real.

One night while resting in bed, thinking all kinds of crazy thoughts. I began to speak to God.

I said, "God, if you're real and there is really a devil, I want you to sit on one shoulder and the devil sit on the other. Prove it!" What a bold move, right? NO! It was stupid to challenge God like that!

Thankfully, He's abundantly compassionate, understanding, and kind. The thing was, I did believe God was 100% real, I just didn't know him, I only knew about him. I continued to think that the devil or hell was nothing more than a fairy tale. Well, on this particular night, God showed me just how real both He and the enemy of my soul really are.

Within a second of asking God to prove it, I immediately felt pain in the shoulder that the devil was sitting on! After realizing what just happened, I began to cry out, "Okay... I believe! I believe! Please God, just show me what I have to live for!"

Suddenly, I saw many orbs of bright white light circled above me. There were so many, I instinctively knew I was in the presence of angels! At first, I thought they had come to get me and that I was going to die. Instead, peace flooded my being. From my bed I could see into my daughter's bedroom across the hall.

I saw a very tall angel standing at the foot of my 3-year-old's bed! The angel was pointing his finger towards my baby girl. The light that came off the angel was not like the brightness of a light bulb or sunlight. It was a different kind of bright white light.

The silhouette angel was shaped in the form of a very tall and slender man. I knew without any conversation that the angel was letting me know my child needed me! Immediately I kicked all the crazy thoughts out of my dying heart. I realized it wasn't about me anymore. My inner pain had to be pushed aside. That's not always an easy thing to do when your heart is involved, but I realized that my daughter's heart and life were more important. She was the reason I had to live and I knew it.

The thought of ending my life was the most selfish thought I could have considered! All I was doing was thinking about myself. After realizing what was happening, I got up and went into my baby girl's room. I brought her back into the bed with me and held her so tight! I felt more peace than I had ever experienced. I cuddled her and she remained sleeping next to me and I soon fell asleep peacefully as well.

Later that night my husband came home from work. I woke up and began to tell him what had happened. He didn't believe a word I said! The next morning the sound of my doorbell ringing woke me up. Surprisingly enough, it was my parents and grandmother. It was very odd, because they had never visited me since we relocated. I began to tell them my experience, but they said, "God doesn't allow an ordinary girl to see angels."

The truth is, God can have one or many angels appear to anyone if

He chooses to! It doesn't matter what denomination, color or creed the person is. Angels are ministering spirits sent by God to assist the believer.

At any rate, my family thought I was hallucinating. I find that amusing now, but I didn't then!

The angelic visitation with the surrounding orbs and the tall angel was etched into my memory for life. No one on earth could tell me that experience wasn't real. After the angelic encounter, and with all the talk and criticism I received, I felt shut down even more. I was so hurt that no one believed me. In some ways it angered me.

My parents suggested that we have dinner with them later in the day. It was nothing more than a set-up to get me to a doctor. They convinced me to go to the doctor to get something to help me rest because of my thoughts. They deceived me, they did not take me to doctor's office, but instead took me took me to a hospital to see a psychiatrist!

I felt so betrayed by my family. I didn't share my experience with the doctor, why would I? My own family didn't believe me. I was alone without the support of anyone! Betrayal from my family was what I received. I was brought to a stranger for help because they didn't believe I could have seen angels. In addition to that, I honestly felt let down by God. *I cried out to Him, "God, I called on you and this is what I get."* For the next four months I ran from Him, not to Him.

Less than two months later we moved back to our hometown. I was homesick and needed to be closer to family and friends. My angelic visitation was now months passed and I didn't care to talk about it with anyone.

After getting to know Jesus I knew I had to forgive my family for the betrayal I felt. I don't think they ever truly realized how badly they had hurt me, or the extent of what I had actually gone through. because of it. Not just the visitation, but all that my heart was enduring previously.

Let's look at what a few Scriptures say about angels.

Are not all angels ministering spirits sent to serve those who will inherit salvation? (Hebrews 1:14)

Angels are spiritual beings created by God. We do know that the Bible refers to angels in numerous ranks and divisions. Lucifer or Satan is the leader of one-third of the evil or fallen angels known as demons (see Job 1:6), *while the remaining two-thirds are holy angels and are under the authority of God.*

From what I know about angels, like human beings, they have been created to serve the Creator. They have many duties: I'll share just a few scriptures, though there are many more.

(a) for praise and worship:

Psalm 148:2
Praise him, all his angels; *praise him, all his heavenly hosts.*

(b) to bring messages from God to mankind:

Luke 1:26
Now in the sixth month the ***angel Gabriel was sent from God*** *to a city in Galilee called Nazareth, to a virgin engaged to a man whose name was Joseph, of the descendants of David; and the virgin's name was Mary. And coming in, he said to her, "Greetings, favored one! The Lord is with you.*

Luke 2:8-11 (NIV)
*8 And there were shepherds living out in the fields nearby, keeping watch over their flocks at night. 9 **An angel of the Lord appeared to them,** and the glory of the Lord shone around them, and they were terrified. 10 But the angel said to them, "Do not be afraid. I bring you good news that will cause great joy for all the people. 11 Today in the town of David a Savior has been born to you; he is the Messiah, the Lord.*

(c) to provide for God's people;

Psalm 91:11 (NIV)
*11 For he will **command his angels concerning you to guard you in all your ways;***

Matthew 4:10-11 New (NIV)

[10] *Jesus said to him, "Away from me, Satan! For it is written: 'Worship the Lord your God, and serve him only.'[a]"*

[11] *Then the devil left him, and **angels came and attended him**.*

(d) to protect God's people;

"Matthew 2:13 (NIV)

[13] *When they had gone, an **angel of the Lord appeared to Joseph in a dream**. "Get up," he said, "take the child and his mother and escape to Egypt. Stay there until I tell you, for Herod is going to search for the child to kill him."*

Daniel 6:22 (NIV)

Daniel, servant of the living God, has your God, whom you serve continually, been able to rescue you from the lions?" [21] *Daniel answered, "May the king live forever!* [22] ***My God sent his angel, and he shut the mouths of the lions.***

(e) to carry out God's will;

Acts 12:7 (NIV)

[7] ***Suddenly an angel of the Lord appeared*** *and a light shone in the cell.* ***He struck Peter*** *on the side and woke him up. "Quick, get up!" he said, and the chains fell off Peter's wrists.*

f) to punish God's enemies, including Satan.

Psalms 78:49

"He cast upon them the fierceness of his anger, wrath, and indignation, and trouble, by sending evil angels among them."

There are many scripture references to cover about the angelic and how God has them here for our guidance and protection.

I am thankful for my angelic visitation. This reason and several others are the reason why I not only believe in the supernatural, but I believe God, angels, demons, and Satan are all real, but only one is **Supreme**, **All Knowing, and Omnipresent** – God.

Chapter

5

Not Just Any Lunch

It was January 1981, a few months after my angelic experience. Thankfully, we had moved back to my hometown. I was invited to have lunch with my aunt, cousins and a couple of their friends.

This wasn't just any lunch, but a lunch planned specifically for me; only I didn't know it then. We were all sitting around the table eating, laughing, and having a good time. They were sharing things about God with excitement. I felt that the lunch was a set-up, deliberately done I'm sure. I'm so grateful for that! They showed me love by sharing more of who Jesus is with me. *That day my life was turned around!*

These beautiful ladies later highlighted the need that I verbally make Jesus my Lord and Savior. I had accepted Jesus in my heart as a child but I didn't really get to know Him. They informed me that the only way to be reconciled back to the Father was through Jesus, the Son of God who died for my sins. Without Jesus I couldn't go to heaven. He's the only door and the only way to be restored to the Father. The whole time I thought I was going to heaven just because I was a Catholic. Wrong!

My life was absent of peace, which was my first red flag. But that afternoon I learned something special. The ladies shared that **I needed to know my Savior.** I needed Him to heal my heart, and to baptize (*fill*) me with His spirit. I was walking around with a broken heart, yet I had done nothing about it, nor did I know how to do anything about it. I just felt so unhappy inside. Not only was my heart broken, it was becoming hard and callous. Unforgiveness will do that. I was wounded in many ways and my soul needed to be healed.

During the lunch we were all having such a good time. I remember watching the ladies laughing and full of joy. They made me realize that I was missing something and I wanted what they had. It was that afternoon that I was introduced to Jesus in a much different way. In prayer, we asked the Lord to heal my heart and to *fill* me with His presence. Within minutes, I felt His company in such a way that I too became full of joy! It's hard to describe what I felt. All that pain inside seem to be lifted in a magical way. It was like I was dead and empty but then I became alive.

After we ate and prayed, a funny thing happened. The room was full of joy following my surrender to God. One of the ladies had gotten so excited that she left the house without her shoes! She came running back inside when she realized she walked out the door in her socks!

I must say, it's an exhilarating feeling that takes over when you see an individual come in broken and then leave full of JOY! That individual was me! The excitement that the ladies felt that day was like seeing a new baby being born. I believe 100% that Jesus was the one behind the planning of this lunch. No one can come to the Lord unless the Spirit of God draws them.

John 6:44 where Jesus declares,
   "No one can come to Me unless the Father who sent Me draws him, and I will raise him up on the last day."

The following week, we all met for lunch again. Go figure. This time around we were going to have a designated time for prayer afterwards. The conversation at the table was about hearing God's voice. Some of them were sharing different things that the Lord had spoken to them about in the past and were excited to get into prayer, expecting Him to speak again.

Later, everyone found a quiet spot and got comfortable. Some of us simply positioned ourselves on our knees and bowed over, while others prayed standing up. It didn't matter the position. We began to pray and seek God's presence. I pressed in. I wanted so bad to hear His voice, but I heard nothing. I kept asking and praying. Still nothing! The prayer went on for some time as I prayed about generic stuff. Back then, I didn't know what to pray for, nevertheless, I wasn't giving up.

When our prayer time had come to an end, everyone started to get up from where they were. We came together and some of the women began to share what they felt The Holy Spirit was saying to them. I had nothing to share, but I believe God heard my heart's cry to hear His voice because He spoke a word to my Aunt just for me! He specifically gave her a prophetic word for me. He had her write it down and give it to me after the prayer. I was astonished. The word that was given to my aunt, on my behalf, ended up being for me and my husband. All this prophecy stuff was never taught in the church that I grew up in, but I discovered that it is very scriptural.

—— My First Prophetic Word: February 4, 1981 ——

"I have a mighty ministry for them. As they seek me so shall they find me. Jennifer will know herself in a new way and will be at peace with this knowledge. I made her. I know her. I love her. I say come as you are. My desires will soon be yours" (only partial part of prophecy shared).

To this day, I do see myself in a new way and peace is my reward. My desires are to please the Lord in every way possible. It's my desire for everyone to feel the love and peace that I feel. I was so excited with the prophecy that I chose to explore the significance of the first sentence: I have a mighty ministry for them.

The word "mighty" means possessing great and impressive power or strength, especially on account of size [powerful · forceful]. The word "ministry" is from the Greek word *diakoneo*, meaning "to serve" or *douleuo*, meaning "to serve as a slave." Now in the New Testament, ministry is seen as a service to God and to other people in His name. Jesus provided the pattern for the Christian ministry—He came, not to receive service, but to give it.

Ministry also means the unique Christian correlation of three conceptions: leadership, service, and gifts. Leadership depends on service, and service is reliant on the possession and recognition of special "gifts" which were the evidence of the presence and power of the Spirit of God within the community.

As a member of my community, it's my reasonable service to give my life and to serve the One who died in order for me to have true life in the first place. I am not my own. Serving Christ comes with a price.

The fact that Jesus could take someone like me who was broken, insecure, full of anxiety, fear and stress is beyond my understanding. Then, on top of that, heal my heart and fill me with His joy, hope, and peace. This new me was a total miracle!

As I journal this, I feel the fullness of His love! His mighty work had already begun within me in order for His "mighty ministry" to be accomplished. It is His ministry. Only the Spirit of God could fulfill the description of those two words. I *get to* co-labor and participate getting blessed in the midst of what God wants to achieve. **Bottom line, I'm called to co-labor with Christ and serve others.**

He is changing me from the inside out and I feel it. Anything good that comes from me is His doing! The Lord gets *all* the credit for the good in my life. Whatever good that is seen in me is Christ in me.

One of my favorite passages comes from Philippians 1:6 which says, **"He who began a good work in you is faithful to complete what He has begun."** Since the beginning of my born-again salvation experience, I've held on to that Scripture. There is no way I could keep myself clean without Him! I have had so much pain, muck, and mire in me that it could have only been the Spirit of God that saved me from myself! Knowing that the Spirit of God is the one who keeps me safe is my assurance. He will never leave me or forsake me.

If you didn't already know, Jesus is a mastermind. He knows just what to touch in your heart to bring you the healing you need. **He doesn't plow you down and make you feel ugly about your sin.** *He's full of love and grace. When you get to know Him you simply fall in love with Him and my lunch buddies knew that as truth.* I couldn't wait to get to know Him more. God is spirit, but He is also a perfect person in every way. Receiving Jesus is becoming born again. **Born of the Spirit.**

You must worship God is Spirit and in truth. (John 4:24)

Jesus answered, "Very truly I tell you, no one can enter the kingdom of God unless they are **born of water and the Spirit.** Flesh gives birth to flesh, but the Spirit gives birth to spirit. You should not be surprised at my saying, *'You must be born again.'* The wind blows wherever it pleases. You hear its sound, but you cannot tell where it comes from or where it is going. So, it is with everyone born of the Spirit."

I remember asking The Holy Spirit to help me grasp this. Within my understanding, this is the interpretation I received:

The Spirit of God is like the wind. You can't see it, yet it's there. His wind is like the fresh breath of God Himself. When God breathes His wind or His breath in you, it becomes a new life, the same way it did when He breathed life into Adam in the beginning. It's spiritual!

After lunch that day, I began a close walk with God, keeping my Aunt and my cousins close. I have learned that it's important to hang with like-minded people who walk strong in their faith. This is called Godly accountability. The world has so much to offer, but it will leave you empty. What it offers is only a temporary satisfaction.

The gratification of material things or worldly success will leave you empty on the inside because it doesn't fill your spirit; only God can fill that.

My desire is to have God's presence deep within me every day because of this miraculous peace and joy that I feel. No one on earth can fill my heart this way. I feel His love deeper now than ever before. His love is so deep and so real. What amazes me the most is that He will never leave me! I cannot surprise Him with anything because He knows all and yet He has never abandoned me!

He's more than my best friend, He's part of me now. He's in me, and I'm in Him. To Love Him means I love myself. If I hate myself, I don't love or even know Him.

Chapter

6

Three in One

It took a long while, but I'm learning to discern the difference between the Trinity. I've learned that the Father, the Son, and The Holy Spirit are the same yet different.

I can tell when I'm hearing from the Father (who I call Papa). I feel so much love and trust for Him. When I feel lonely or upset, I simple picture myself at His feet with my head in His lap and his gentle hand stroking my hair … or I'm simply sitting in His lap like his little girl with my head leaning on His chest. He's so very comforting. He speaks with so much wisdom; it's undeniable. My knowing that He's got my back is super-natural.

I also know that as his child he will do what's necessary to keep me protected, even if it hurts. His discipline is sometimes painful when I persist on having my own way. I do know that what He does is for my own good. I'm so protected, covered and cared for. It's so real I feel that I'm daddy's little girl. He would do anything for me, in fact He did. He gave me Jesus.

Jesus His only Son, is my Savior and absolute best friend and my LORD. He's perfect in every way. He is the Righteous One, the one who took on my sin, and the sins of the world for that matter. He covered me with His righteousness so I could be restored back to the father again. I'm so very grateful to Him. Without Him we would never be able to be reconciled back to God. His love and forgiveness give us our freedom. I feel at times, that I am walking hand in hand with Jesus having conversations about anything and everything. I can expose anything to Him and **never feel ashamed**. He knows it all anyway. He covered all my sins with His blood atonement. Funny thing, He always seems to answer my questions with a question. In doing so, I discover the answer. At times I feel when He's actually fighting my battles, **with Him I can't lose.** He's the Lion of Judea, My Prince of Peace, He's the everlasting God. He has taken victory in every area and because of His Victory…. I'm always protected and safe, He is UNSTOPPABLE! What's so very cool, is when the enemy looks at me, he now runs…. because he sees JESUS IN ME!

Holy Spirit, well He is God's Spirit inside me. The inner witness who guides and comforts me, He never leaves me, He restores that which was broken in me, He never pushes or insists on his own way but teaches, and corrects me keeping me on the right path. His presence is so fulfilling and so tangible that He cannot be denied. The Holy Spirit is the one who speaks for me even when I don't know what to say. And the comfort that I feel from him is like non-other. No one can comfort me like The Holy Spirit. When I've done something wrong, and I have felt that I've grieved Him; I know it. It's the worst feeling in the world, I don't ever want to do that again. What's amazing is he doesn't stop with me; through me he wants to touch so many others. He speaks with a non-threatening gentle voice. He wants everyone to know Him and his goodness. He is the fulfillment of life itself. Without Him, you're not really living, you are simply existing. I don't want to just exist; I want to live fulfilled, no longer empty but thriving with His breath (Spirit) inside of me.

My heart and their heart all as ONE. Their love goes deep within me. It's so overwhelming! I feel so full at times and I can't believe that it's my heart. Throughout several points in my life, I have hated myself. I had the awful feelings of self-rejection, emptiness and pain before I met the Lord in three persons.

The only way to the Father is through his Son Jesus. He is the only doorway to the Father. There is no other way.

Jesus explains that no man can come unless the Father draws him (John 6:65).

The natural man has no desire to come to him because his mind is darkened by the enemy of this world. Without Him no man can approach the Father. The Holy Spirit convicts us of our sinful nature and our need for a Savior.

But it is only through help of Holy Spirit, the very breath and life of God, for all this freedom and peace to become possible.

God is creator of the Universe and everything in it. Jesus is the Son, the actual seed of God, and The Holy Spirit is the very breath of Life .... Are all One in the same. The three–in–one from the beginning had a beautiful and glorious plan. They wanted to personally enjoy their creation, therefore the three of them created man in their image and anticipated man's fellowship. God knew that His creation would need a means of rescue one day because they would fall into a deep hole of disobedience, which is sin. And what I've learned about being rescued and returning to true fellowship with God and others is this, **it requires us to be born–again.**

Chapter

7

Who is Satan?

The devil known as Satan, and also referred to as Lucifer. He is a fallen angel who was an arch angel in heaven over the ministry of music. He was created even before man was created. He was made beautiful and very intelligent, the most beautiful of all the angels. The Bible records God's Spirit speaking through Ezekiel saying:

You were in Eden, the garden of God; every precious stone adorned you: carnelian, chrysolite and emerald, topaz, onyx and jasper, lapis lazuli, turquoise and beryl. Your settings and mountings were made of gold; on the day you were created they were prepared. You were anointed as a guardian cherub, for so I ordained you. You were on the holy mount of God; you walked among the fiery stones. You were blameless in your ways from the day you were created till wickedness was found in you. Through your widespread trade you were filled with violence, and you sinned. So, I drove you in disgrace from the mount of God, and I expelled you, guardian cherub, from among the fiery stones. Your heart became proud on account of your beauty, and you corrupted your wisdom because of your splendor. So, I threw

you to the earth; I made a spectacle of you before kings. You
were anointed as a guardian cherub, for so I ordained you.
(28:13-17, NIV)

Major problem! Lucifer had pride in his heart because of his beauty. He saw how all the angels were worshiping God and he wanted that for himself. He wanted a god-like adoration, therefore he led many of the angels away from worshiping the one true God and appointed himself as supreme. I don't know that I will ever understand that. How could any of the angels choose to follow Satan over God? I reason that the enemy is so cleverly made that we really need The Holy Spirit to expose his doings. There is no way a created being can become greater than his Creator.

As the story is told, God cast Satan and his following angel's known as demons out of heaven! Since then, the devil has roamed the earth working very hard to destroy man! Without God, every individual is an open target for the destruction of the enemy. He has a great deal of persuasion over those who follow their own selfish ways and not God's.

You're either serving God or you're not. Plain and simple. When we fall into the trap of being our own boss, wanting to follow our own selfish ways and desires, it resembles the enemy. Being independent of God is the worst position you could be in, no matter how popular or successful you are.

Do you carry pride in your heart? Are you saying that you are greater than the Creator too? Food for thought.

The devil moves in ranks, similar like the military does. As Satan gives orders to his fallen angels, these thieves will come into our lives only to steal, kill, and destroy. *Jesus, however, has come that we may have life, and have it to the fullest (John 10:10).*

The Bible informs us in *Ephesians 6:12 that our struggle is not against flesh and blood, but against the rulers, authorities, and powers of this dark world and spiritual evil forces in the heavenly realms.*

Realize this before the enemy was cast out of heaven, he stood in the presence of God in all Gods glory. When you're in the presence of God you radiate His Glory. The enemy was beautiful and intelligent. We most definitely need the presence of God to reveal the wiles of the enemy. I'm not trying to bring a shining light upon the enemy, I simply want everyone to realize their need for God to be saved from the enemy. God will instruct you in the way you should go with your obedience.

God knew that man would be schemed by the crafty devil and fall, therefore He made a plan of rescue prior to this event in history even happening.

My grandson Landon asked me, "Why did God create the devil if he knew he would do this? *A very good question, especially coming from a 7-year-old.* Free will was the direct answer I gave him. "We all have free will," I said. "Our relationship with God is by choice. It is not forced. We have the free will to choose between right and wrong. The Lord gave Adam and Eve specific instructions to obey and they chose to disobey. We always get into trouble when we disobey.

Genesis 3

Now the serpent was more crafty than any of the wild animals the Lord God had made. He said to the woman, "Did God really say, 'You must not eat from any tree in the garden'?"

² The woman said to the serpent, "We may eat fruit from the trees in the garden, ³ but God did say, 'You must not eat fruit from the tree that is in the middle of the garden, and you must not touch it, or you will die.'"

⁴ "You will not certainly die," the serpent said to the woman. ⁵ "For God knows that when you eat from it your eyes will be opened, and you will be like God, knowing good and evil."

⁶ When the woman saw that the fruit of the tree was good for food and pleasing to the eye, and also desirable for gaining wisdom, she took some and ate it. She also gave some to her husband, who was with her, and he ate it. ⁷ Then the eyes of both of them were opened, and they realized they were naked; so, they sewed fig leaves together and made coverings for themselves. Gen 3:1-7

The Lie from the enemy, "When you eat from the tree you will be like God. **Adam and Eve were already made in the image of God**. He also said they would not die. They did die, spiritually speaking. They were separated from God and needed what only the Son of God could bring…they needed The Holy Spirit to make them spiritually alive again. Deception of the enemy brought spiritual death.

Adam and Eve were the first man and woman on the earth and the devil managed to deceive them into doing something God told them not to do. He twisted the word, causing them to sin against God.

From the point of Adam and Eve eating the fruit from the Tree of Knowledge of Good and Evil, the both of them ended up being under a curse from God. The Lord knew all this would happen and discipline would be needed. Thankfully, the reverse was already in place to save us. **Nothing gets past God. He knows all; from beginning to end.** God doesn't want his people to be robots. He wants lovers with a free will! People that whole heartedly have a relationship with Him to receive his love and love Him back. Without knowing God, you really don't know love.

The father knew that the intelligence and trickery of the devil had to be crushed, so God sent the seed of himself to personally take care of the enemy. He himself placed his seed inside a virgin ….

See Matthew 1:23, Luke 1:27, Isaiah 7:14, Matthew 1:18-25.

The Creator is absolutely more intelligent than that of his creation. It doesn't matter how smart he made Lucifer, the Father simply played his hand and outsmarted the enemy and *will each and every time*. The Almighty God knew all along that he would need to prepare a sacrifice for the redemption of man.

The Father's plan…. His only Son, Jesus who is God was with the Father from the beginning. Jesus is the Word. He laid his deity down and became the sacrifice to reconcile mankind back to Himself at the appointed time. This sacrifice was and is perfect in every way.

The Word Becomes Flesh

[14] And the Word became flesh and dwelt among us, and we beheld His glory, the glory as of the only begotten of the Father, full of grace and truth. John 1:14 (NKJV).

The Sin-Bearing Messiah

53 Who has believed our report?
And to whom has the arm of the LORD been revealed?
[2] For He shall grow up before Him as a tender plant,
And as a root out of dry ground.
He has no [a]form or [b]comeliness;
And when we see Him,
There is no [c]beauty that we should desire Him.
[3] He is despised and [d]rejected by men,
A Man of [e]sorrows and acquainted with [f]grief.
And we hid, as it were, *our* faces from Him;
He was despised, and we did not esteem Him.

[4] Surely He has borne our [g]griefs
And carried our [h]sorrows;
Yet we [i]esteemed Him stricken,
[j]Smitten by God, and afflicted.
[5] But He *was* wounded[k] for our transgressions,
He was [l]bruised for our iniquities;
The chastisement for our peace *was* upon Him,
And by His stripes[m] we are healed.
[6] All we like sheep have gone astray;

We have turned, every one, to his own way;
And the LORD [n]has laid on Him the iniquity of us all.

7 He was oppressed and He was afflicted,
Yet He opened not His mouth;
He was led as a lamb to the slaughter,
And as a sheep before its shearers is silent,
So He opened not His mouth.
8 He was taken from [o]prison and from judgment,
And who will declare His generation?
For He was cut off from the land of the living;
For the transgressions of My people He was stricken.
9 And [p]they made His grave with the wicked—
But with the rich at His death,
Because He had done no violence,
Nor *was any* deceit in His mouth.

10 Yet it pleased the LORD to [q]bruise Him;
He has put *Him* to grief.
When You make His soul an offering for sin,
He shall see *His* seed, He shall prolong *His* days,
And the pleasure of the LORD shall prosper in His hand.
11 [r]He shall see the labor of His soul, *and* be satisfied.
By His knowledge My righteous Servant shall justify many,
For He shall bear their iniquities.
12 Therefore I will divide Him a portion with the great,
And He shall divide the [s]spoil with the strong,
Because He poured out His soul unto death,
And He was numbered with the transgressors,
And He bore the sin of many,
And made intercession for the transgressors. (Isaiah 53 NKJ)

Behold the Lamb of God who humbled Himself! The Creator of all things loves us so much that He humbled Himself enough to leave heaven and come to earth just to rescue humanity. Can you grasp what has been done? We are already victorious with Him! The enemy of your soul will have frequent wins if you are living your life without God's covering. The power of His Spirit in you is the secret weapon that covers you. It's His Spirit inside you that makes you born again!

Satan, the enemy of our soul, is very intelligent and out to destroy you and your family. One of his biggest tricks is to cause you to believe that he doesn't exist. Satan wants you to believe that he is a fairytale.

He's also an expert at deceiving people into believing that there is no God. Please understand that the one life that you have is being plotted against. The enemy knows that he is doomed for hell, but his goal is to take you with him.

Chapter

8

Faith Verses Fear

Like a magnet, faith and fear are two opposing forces. Yes, *forces*! They are both **very real and powerful**. Both faith and fear project things into the future. I can tell you this because I have experienced and operated in both. Not proud to say that I have operated in fear, but now I'm grateful because I get opportunities to help free others.

I believe, in all honesty, the devil made a huge mistake by attacking me with fear. The spirit of fear is now scared of me. I can smell fear from a mile away. There is a healthy and godly fear...but it's one of respect towards the creator, not one that causes anxiety and stress.

When I first became a Christian, I couldn't put the Bible down. I was drawn to know about this God who I had just given my life to. I wanted to know all I could about Him. While reading my Bible one night, I came across this verse in Proverbs:

The fear of the Lord is the beginning of knowledge, but fools despise wisdom and instruction. (1:7, NIV)

That night as I got comfortable on my pillow, I talked to the Lord and asked Him a question from earlier that day. "Lord, how can I fear you when I don't know you?" The Lord waited until I was quiet enough to hear Him.

Just as I closed my eyes, I saw a set of eyes swoop across in front of me! Immediately, I understood what that verse meant. You see, when I was a child, all my dad had to do was give me a certain look with his eyes and I knew he meant business. I had an **awesome respect for that look**. It wasn't a scared feeling, but a respectful feeling! I was fully aware of my dad's good heart. I knew that if I obeyed him, then all would be well. But if I didn't, then that was another story. My dad never wanted me to lack anything good, but he reminded me often that the choices I made were always mine.

A Spirit of Fear and I Saw It!

Back when I was a newbie to all the Christianity stuff, I didn't know or understand much. All I knew was that I had fallen in love with Jesus, therefore I told everyone about Him. The devil did not like me doing that one bit though. So of course, he tried to stop me.

One night I was lying in bed when I became paralyzed with fear. It gripped me so strongly that I couldn't speak. I was trying to call on Jesus, but I couldn't even blurt a sound out of my mouth. Instead, I called His name in my heart. Then suddenly, I witnessed a vision of a falling net appear above me. The net caught this spirit of fear in mid-air! It was as if the ceiling opened up and the net dropped down. With the net the Lord caught this evil spirit. It was a dark, military green and shaped like a human figure fighting to get out. I was shocked to see that this spirit was so small. The fear lifted off me the second I saw the net catch it. I said out loud, "I was afraid of that?" It was so minor and non-threatening, yet I was paralyzed by it. I thank God for giving me eyes to see in the spirit. The Lord rescued me, all I had to do was call on him! He was right there with me the whole time.

For years that evil spirit caused me to believe falsely. It has shown up in different ways throughout my life, causing me stress and doubt, but, with the help of The Holy Spirit, I overcame the enemy's lies that I had previously believed. **What I believed was exactly what I got**.

As a man thinks in his heart so is he. (Proverbs 23:7 NIV)

You become exactly what you believe about yourself. Believing the enemy's lies was my biggest battle, but I soon realized that lying and deceiving was all he could do.

Since then I have learned, in Christ I have all authority over the enemy. *I simply needed to understand my identity and know who I belong to.*

As mentioned, fear comes in different ways. There is fear and there is a spirit of fear. There was a time that the spirit of fear was destroying me. Not only was it tormenting me, but everyone around me was being impacted. All of this was because I believed the lies that the enemy was putting into my mind. The demon spirit was so deceptive throughout specific times of my life that I thought it was God who I feared. I recall trembling on my knees asking God why I feared Him in this way. How could a sold-out believer battle fear like *that*?

I pressed into God's presence relentlessly by not giving up. I was afraid to be without Him. Thankfully, because of my faith in His Word I was able to win the **battle in my mind!** Fear had me full of doubt, anxiety, sleeplessness, depression, high-blood pressure, paranoia, and the need for medication. I went without sleep for days and, I was out of commission. I then had to medicate to get sleep. I was so ashamed of what was happening to me. I was doing all that a Christian knew how to do. Shame, another thing the enemy brings.

I remember renouncing the enemy, praying, reading God's Word, and worshiping, and yet at times, I was still operating in fear. Why and what was I doing wrong? I was a dedicated Christian, believing and trusting in the Lord. So, I thought! **In all reality, a believer is unable to walk in both trust and fear at the same time. That is being double minded.** And as the truth is told, I was literally a double-minded Christian for a number of years. Unfortunately, so many believers are. I learned that I needed to renounce being double-minded. It was a demon! Resist the enemy and he will FLEE! The whole time I thought it was me. The world needs to know what they battle! It's so vital to stay close to God, get to know HIM and you become unstoppable with HIM.

One day, while I was showering, I felt an evil presence come into the room… it was standing on the outside of the shower door. I could sense the evil spirit was present. I felt it! This particular spirit came to bring me fear again, but instead of giving into its foolishness, I began to sing songs about the blood of Jesus instead. Within a couple of minutes it left. The enemy hates songs about the blood. It's an easy way to win. I sang until it left. I took victory!

The Word of God says, *"Submit yourself then to God, resist the devil and he will flee from you" (James 4:7).*

As believers, we don't have to fight so much once we learn who we are in Christ. When we learn how to fight and look to Jesus rather than the enemy, we begin to walk with the **authority of God.** The enemy isn't afraid of you, **BUT he *is* afraid of God *in* you!** What you focus on grows bigger whether it is fear or faith. Unfortunately, I was looking down at fear and trying to escape it instead of looking up at God. I have since learned to focus on Jesus, the Victorious One. It wasn't until this point that I became fully victorious!

I remember the day I was delivered from the spirit of fear I was at a women's conference. The guest speaker began to share her testimony and to my surprise she shared that *her biggest battle was overcoming fear.* Compared to my occurrences, she had battled fear in a different way; nonetheless, it was the same spirit. She made it clear that she felt led to repent of fear! *Wow. Repent?!* I thought. The whole time I was rebuking and renouncing fear. That was the first time I had heard to repent of fear. The moment I repented for being fearful I literally felt the chains fall off of my ankles. Fear can paralyze us and can stop us from seeing truth. It can stop you from walking by faith and receiving freedom.

Remember, you can't operate in fear and faith at the same time. It's impossible. We will believe one or the other. Fear is the exact opposite of faith. By God's grace, I'm no longer a slave to fear! The reverence of God is the only fear I want to have. The Bible says,

> *"The fear of the Lord is the beginning of wisdom; all who follow his precepts **have good understanding**" (Psalm 111:10) NIV*

Simply put, this verse teaches that the fear of God is foundational to true wisdom. All other types of fear are crippling methods which keep us from becoming who God created us to be. Many other passages throughout the Bible talk about the fear of the Lord such as:

> *"The fear of the Lord is the beginning of knowledge, but fools despise wisdom and discipline." (Proverbs 1:7, NIV)*
>
> *"The fear of the Lord is a fountain of life, turning a man from the snares of death." (Proverbs 14:27, NIV)*
>
> *"The fear of the Lord teaches a man wisdom, and humility comes before honor." (Proverbs 15:33)*

In the Bible the word translated "fear" can mean several things. It can refer to the terror that one feels in a frightening situation, and it can mean respect in the way a servant fears his master and serves him faithfully. As believers we want to practice the latter.

> *"Now fear the Lord and serve him with all faithfulness."* (Joshua 24:14)
>
> *"**There is no fear in love. But perfect love drives out fear,** because fear has to do with punishment. The one who fears is not made perfect in love. God is Love!" (1 John 4:18)*

By getting to know God—who is Love, I became FREE

"Love is patient, love is kind. It does not envy, it does not boast, it is not proud. It is not rude, it is not self-seeking, it is not easily angered, it keeps no record of wrongs. Love does not delight in evil but rejoices with the truth. It always protects, always trusts, always hopes, always perseveres. Love never fails." (1 Corinthians 13:4-8)

God's love is so unstoppable. He will yield at nothing to ensure that you are drawn to Him. He wants to give you all that is good. When you're in covenant with Him, what is His becomes yours too. Relationships take work and you have to give attention to the one you want to be with. It's no different with Jesus. He wants to spend time with us. And if you didn't already know, He's waiting for us.

He was waiting on me!

The verse in Daniel 6:10 is a great example of prayer. Daniel got down on his knees and prayed three times a day, giving thanks to his God. So, I began to do this too and honor the Lord and to get to know Him more. There was one day when I was coming home in a hurry around noon and I wanted to meet with the Lord. As I walked into the room with my hands full of groceries, **I *felt* God's presence** waiting on me. He was sitting in the chair waiting for me to get there.

I felt so overwhelmed that He (Almighty God) was waiting on me. That's how much He wants to be with us. He wants fellowship and intimacy with us more than we can imagine. You cannot have a thriving relationship with someone you don't spend time with. God just so happens to be the most important "someone" in your life. He desires a bride and a groom type of relationship.

Before the foundation of the earth, God has longed for a passionate, holy and eternal love story with human beings. We were designed for fellowship and love. But let it be known that truly loving an invisible God does takes faith.

Always choose faith.

Chapter

9

Filled with His Spirit

I wasn't alone anymore. My new journey was exciting and full of joy. I couldn't get enough of the presence of God. Attending the small, spirit-filled church was much different than the large Catholic Church that I grew up in. This new one had people speaking in tongues which at first was so weird to me. I'll share more about tongues later, but I honestly thought these people were strange and off-the-wall. Then I realized they were normal, happy, and loving just like myself.

It was presumptuous of me to think they were the crazy ones. The more I attended, the more I wanted God's presence. There was a feeling in this church that I had not felt before and I loved it. The following month, I became what many call **"Filled with the Spirit."** Boy, what a surprise that was! My husband and I found ourselves running to the church every time the doors were opened. We were so alive!

One Sunday afternoon, we were at my in-law's house for a Sunday barbecue when we realized later that evening church was about to start. The time had slipped away from us and we only had a half hour before service started. So, with no time to go home and clean ourselves up, we went to church in our t-shirts, shorts, and sandals. Come as you are, right?

The pastor took notice of our hunger for God and asked us to come up front to lead prayer for the offering and the prayer petitions.

I was just getting started with my private prayers so I was not at all used to praying out loud, and especially not publicly. My husband quickly grabbed me by the hand and pulled me up to my feet to go forth.

While my husband was praying for the offering, I was asking God under my breath to pray through me when it came my turn to pray. Honestly, I was scared to death. But, let me tell you… Wow! He did *just* that! His presence filled me instantly. All of a sudden, I felt like someone turned on a light within. My eyes felt like they were on fire. When I opened my mouth and started to pray, words were coming out that I had never even thought of. It seemed so powerful, the people started clapping and rejoicing. I put my hands over my eyes because I felt God's presence so strong, it felt as if it was a fiery presence.

There was a lady in the front row who tapped me and asked if I knew what was happening. I never felt anything so powerful before. "God's presence is all over you," she said. "I believe He has just filled you with His Spirit."

When I asked God to pray through me, it was my invitation for Him to fill me with His spirit. All I knew was the feeling I felt was nothing that I had ever felt before. It was electrifying. No one on earth could tell me that God wasn't real! This wasn't just words; it was an experience of **HIS PRESENCE!** The inner witness was so undeniable. It's **HIS POWER!**

On that day, my journey began. I was happy to serve God. Nothing in life was as real as His presence inside of me. All I know is that the God of the universe is a living spirit. He who created me also lives inside of me. You might be wondering; *you were filled with what?* Yes, I was filled with a new spirit. God's Spirit.

I will give you a new heart and put a new spirit in you; I will remove from you your heart of stone and give you a heart of flesh. And I will put my Spirit in you and move you to follow my decrees and be careful to keep my laws. Then you will live in the land I gave your ancestors; you will be my people, and I will be your God. I will save you from all your uncleanness. I will call for the grain and make it plentiful and will not bring famine upon you. (Ezekiel 36:26-29)

"And it shall come to pass afterward, I will pour out my Spirit on all people. Your sons and daughters will prophesy, your old men will dream dreams, your young men will see visions." (Joel 2:28-29 NIV)

This has happened to me! I can't fully express how amazing this is. His power is like electricity flowing through me. There is no denying what I feel is real. To this day, I sense His presence is so very strong at times. I can feel it all throughout my hands, arms, on my face, in my back, and even on my head. Not always everywhere at once. He can touch me anyway He chooses. To God be the glory! When you invite Him in, you get His Spirit! At times, my heart feels so full. I can't explain it. His presence enables us to walk in peace, hope, and joy. Something I didn't have much of before being filled. There are times that He's completely silent or doesn't let me feel His presence. But I know this is a faith walk and He's always with me.

If your heart has ever been in a low place, ask the Lord to fill you with His presence. Surrender your pain and your past to Him. Let His presence *fill* you today!

It's a very simple prayer.

"Jesus, I invite you into my heart. Please forgive me of my sins and fill me with your presence. Become the Lord of my life."

Let's read what happened to the new believers in the New Testament book of Acts.

"When the day of Pentecost came, they were all together in one place. Suddenly a sound like the blowing of a violent

wind came from heaven and filled the whole house where they were sitting. They saw what seemed to be tongues of fire that separated and came to rest on each of them. All of them were filled with The Holy Spirit and began to speak in other tongues as the Spirit enabled them." (v2:1-4)

"For this is that which was spoken by the prophet Joel." (v2:16)

As joyful as I was, the flipside revealed some not so joyful people. A few of members of my family were not so happy that I had become a **born-again believer.** They were Catholic and didn't understand what I was experiencing. They wanted to know why I had left the Catholic religion. My precious grandmother asked in the presence of my parents, Jennifer, why did you forsake the Catholic faith?"

Being a new believer, I stopped in my tracks and remained speechless until seconds later I was comforted by who gave me my answer. "Because I learned the truth," I replied.

One thing I learned during this season was that following Jesus is *not* a religion. He is a person who wants to have a personal relationship with each of us. His whole purpose of dying on the cross as a perfect sacrifice was to reconcile us back with our heavenly Father.

From the beginning, God wanted us to live in harmony and paradise with Him. But when sin entered the world because of disobedience, humanity was disconnected from the Father. This is not at all about religion, but a relationship. I no longer just know Him as just the "Son of God" who died on the cross, but as *my* personal Lord and Savior. All the stories of Christ came to life in a much more personal way as our relationship evolved. It was like my light was turned on and now I was able to see. Jesus said,

"I am the way, the truth, and the life. No one comes to the Father except through me" (John 14:6).

This is such a true statement. Jesus is The Way, The Truth, and The Life.

I wanted to know all of what God had in store for me so I read the Bible every opportunity I had. I was getting to know Him by praying and talking to Him all of the time. I constantly sang praises to God because I was told that He loves our praises. I learned that He loves hearing from me so what better thing to do with my time and energy than to talk to the One who created me. That still amazes me! The Creator of the entire universe wants to spend time with me. He created me and you for fellowship and to be in perfect harmony with Him. One day we will get back to the perfect plan and I can hardly wait. **Don't make a promise to God that you cannot keep. I learned that the hard way.**

It has been decades now since I have decided to walk with the Lord. But let me share how **He scared the sin out of me** in the early days. I wanted to please God in every way possible. On a particular day I made a promise to Him that I didn't keep. I was a cigarette smoker when I first got saved and it was a terrible habit and it took time to get free. So, every time I tried to quit, I failed miserably. One evening I had promised God that I wouldn't smoke the next morning when I woke up. Well, the next day when I got out of bed, I remembered the promise, but my desire for the cigarette overrode my promise to God. I continued to reach for the cigarettes. You would never believe how God got my attention!

Later that night just as soon I went to bed, a Scripture popped up in my mind. I got up to search for that verse to see what He was saying... I didn't know the Bible well at the time, so I had to look in the index to even find what I was looking for. Then I found it!

"When you make a promise to God, don't delay in following through, for God takes no pleasure in fools. Keep all the promises you make to him." (Ecclesiastes 5:4, NIV)

Oh, my Lord! My heart fell after reading it! But it didn't stop there… we had just moved, and I had a twin-size sheet folded in half on a curtain rod to cover a window. Just as I read that scripture, the sheet *flew* off the rod! Talk about being scared! If it had fallen straight down it would have stayed right near the window, instead it flew across the room! It scared me so bad, I hit my knees so fast!

How God delivers a message to us doesn't matter. What matters is why God delivered the message. I quickly repented and never promised anything again! I learned to approach God with *awe.* Like I mentioned earlier, **the fear of God is the beginning of wisdom.** I guess you can say that day was the day I started to receive a bit more revelation on wisdom. And yes, I was scared! **It was the right kind of fear.** Some might say that God's method was a bit harsh, but I feel that He deals with each person differently for a reason. I don't know why He had to make me realize how important my words are to Him. All I know is this: He got my attention!

God is gentle, yet *all* powerful. He is ever present, yet everywhere at once. He is the great I AM. Just like my dad would correct me, my heavenly Father corrects me! The Bible tells us:

"For the Lord corrects those he loves, just as a father corrects a child in whom he delights." (Proverbs 3:12)

By the way, I did quit smoking. But not on my own. I heard from God in a very, very clear way. I was minding my own business when I heard Him speak. It was very unexpected. I wasn't in prayer at the time. I was picking up a cigarette when he spoke. "Lay them down," God said, "before you die a horrible death of cancer before your children." He didn't want my children to see that!

My heart was about to come out of my chest! I knew God's voice and heard Him very clearly. I didn't want my kids to see me suffer a death like that or for them to experience the pain of it. I felt so convicted. I laid on the living room floor and cried out to God for help. I pleaded with Him to take the addiction of nicotine out of me. I knew I couldn't do it unless He removed it from me. And guess what?! He did just that. God delivered me from the poison that was in my lungs. For many days I was being cleansed of nicotine. Every time I blew my nose it was orange. I know…gross! Since then, I feel I can breathe and have more energy.

I want you to understand just how real this actually was. I wanted to quit and I tried so many times but failed. It was over 30 years ago and I have not had any desire for that horrible habit since then. My Savior healed and delivered me of such a tormenting habit; one that I couldn't get free of on my own. Not only was I free, but everyone around me didn't have to suffer that horrible smell or the damaging effects it carried. What an amazing God we serve!

Speaking in Tongues

Another benefit of being in the presence of God's Spirit is the gift of tongues. I had asked Him to fill me with the gift of tongues one day because I wanted everything that the Bible says He has to offer me, including spiritual gifts. While singing praises, I began to speak in an unknown language.

At first, when it happened, I felt that I might have been repeating what I had heard others saying. I doubted if I had actually received the gift of tongues or not. But it was like the doubt I felt was not my thoughts. I believe the doubt came from the enemy. The devil definitely doesn't want me or anyone else to operate in the gift of tongues because of the power of it.

With this gift, God gives us the ability to pray His perfect will. When we pray in tongues, we are allowing God to flow through us and to speak His mysteries. With tongues you allow Him to pray through you. Read what the book of Acts says about the gift of speaking in tongues:

"¹When the Day of Pentecost had fully come; they were all with one accord in one place. ² And suddenly there came a sound from heaven, as of a rushing mighty wind, and it filled the whole house where they were sitting. ³ Then there appeared to them divided tongues, as of fire, and one sat upon each of them. ⁴ And they were all filled with The Holy Spirit and began to speak with other tongues, as the Spirit gave them utterance. (Acts 2:1-4, KJV)

"¹⁷ 'And it shall come to pass in the last days, says God, That I will pour out of My Spirit on all flesh; Your sons and your daughters shall prophesy, your young men shall see visions, your old men shall dream dreams. ¹⁸ And on My men servants I will pour out My Spirit in those days; And they shall prophesy. (Acts 2:17-18, KJV)

³³ Therefore being exalted to the right hand of God, and having received from the Father the promise of Holy Spirit, He poured out this which you now see and hear." (v33, KJV)

Then Peter said unto them, Repent, and be baptized every one of you in the name of Jesus Christ for the remission of sins, and ye shall receive the gift of the Holy Ghost. ³⁹ For the promise is unto you, and to your children, and to all that are afar off, even as many as the Lord our God shall call. (Acts 2:38-39, KJV).

Concerning speaking in tongues, when The Holy Spirit comes upon us, our speech organs become quickened (made alive). We first notice the stammering of our lips (see Isaiah 28:11). We should surrender our thoughts and our tongue to which allows for the Spirit of God to speak through us. The words are foreign to our understanding unless God has also given you or someone else the unique gift of interpreting tongues. Both of these spiritual gifts are a sign of the baptism of The Holy Spirit.

I hope you took good notice of what Acts 2:17 and 18 tells us. We are in the last days and tongues are evidence of The Holy Spirit speaking through the believer. I have had very powerful experiences concerning tongues. I will share two of my speaking in tongues experiences in the upcoming chapter. I do hope this will bless you and encourage you in your faith and hopefully your personal walk as your relationship with the Lord grows.

These stories I tell are so necessary to share because His goodness is in all of them. I pray that my testimonies bring you freedom and anyone else that may need to be free. I am privileged to live in a country where I have the freedom to speak about God and worship Him without hindrance.

Miracles began to happen, and praying in tongues was so necessary. The next story will amaze you...

Chapter

10

Joseph and the 18-Wheeler

Being a new Christian I was learning to ponder and meditate on the Scriptures. I couldn't get a particular scripture out of my mind all day long. ***"The prayers of a righteous man avail much." James 5:16.***

That evening when I came home from work, I heard that verse in my heart as I walked through the front door. While cooking dinner, I heard it again. I walked down the hall toward my bedroom, I heard it once more. At that moment, I realized that God was leading me to pray. I knelt by my bedside and began to pray. I had no idea who or what I was praying for, so I prayed in the spirit, in an "unknown tongue." I had learned that when you pray in tongues it's the Spirit of God who is praying through you.

I asked the Lord to show me who I was praying for. Just then, I had an image of an 18- wheeler! I saw the vision so very clear. Then another vision of emergency lights! Suddenly, I realized I was praying for my brother who drove an 18-wheeler! The flashing red lights were telling me that this prayer was an emergency! I was praying so hard for him; I knew he was in trouble. Then I felt a heaviness in my chest; I didn't understand that and I was scared for him. I called a leader in the church and quickly explained what was happening. She said to keep praying until the heaviness in my chest lifted. She mentioned that God sometimes allows us to feel things that help us pray through.

She confirmed the lights in the vision were for emergency prayer! While praying in tongues, I heard The Holy Spirit saying, "Rise to your feet, and lift your hands towards the heavens." As I did, it felt as if someone plugged me into the electric outlet. A surge of powerful energy flowed through my hands and fingers. Instinctively, I knew exactly how to pray and I found myself commissioning the angels to surround the truck from the north, south, east, and west! They were to bring my brother to safety.

Soon after, I then had another vision. This time I saw the truck pulled over and stopped. The heaviness in my chest lifted and I felt relief. I called the leader back and was telling her all that had happened when all of a sudden, my husband busted through the door yelling at me to hang up the phone! My bedroom door had been ajar and he had been eavesdropping on my phone conversation. This spiritual stuff was all new to both of us. He was very upset and uncomfortable with my conversation. Another reason why he was upset was because he didn't understand spiritual matters.

The next evening my husband and I went to deliver a birthday gift to my brother's son. As we were pulling up to the house to park, my brother drove up in his 18-wheeler. He barely had a chance to turn the truck off when he slid from the cab to the ground shouting, *"Brother-in-law! Brother-in-law! You'll never believe what happened to me last night!" He continued, "I fell asleep behind the wheel and I even saw my face in a casket!"*

WOW… Did my brother just say he was in such a deep sleep that he had a dream? Sometimes dreams can be warnings. In that case, he definitely received the warning! He described many of the same things that my husband overheard me saying on the phone. Just then, my husband's hair stood up on the back of his neck. He realized that I did have a connection in the Spirit for prayer.

I then turned toward my brother and yelled at him because of how scared he had me. I told him what I had experienced. We argued a little about him getting some sleep before driving. His response to me was, "You're spooking me out!"

I share this story to say this, **"The prayers of the righteous do avail much." (James 5:16).**

Thankfully, my brother's life was spared. Not only that, but I am thankful for my firsthand experience on how important speaking in tongues is. Speaking in this unknown language was exactly what was needed to pray for my brother. I would never have known how to pray in such an emergency. Praying in the spirit put me right into the throne room of God. When the Spirit leads things happen! I also learned how to cooperate with the angels to get my brother protected. They move at the word of the Lord. When you're operating in the Spirit, you become the voice of God. His Spirit is operating through your vessel.

Chapter

11

The Gas Tank

One Wednesday night I was getting ready to leave for church. As I was ready to drive away, I noticed that I needed gas. I went back into the house and asked my husband for some gas money. He sarcastically told me, "Ask God for the gas!" Ok, I will! He wasn't happy about my running back and forth to church. So, as I went outside, I said, "God, I need gas, could you please fill my tank? When I got into the car, my tank was full! I ran back inside screaming, "He did it! He did it! He filled my tank!" My husband, of course stunned, looked at me saying, "What?!" He jumped up and ran out with me to look at the gas gauge.

Just as we came out of the door there was a beautiful large and bright rainbow that appeared in the sky above us. I pointed up, saying, "Look, another one of God's promises!" It was God's visible sign and covenant promise to us all that the earth would not end with a flood again as it did with Noah (See Gen 9:12-17).

When my husband looked at the gas gauge his eyes widened very large. Ha! What an amazing God we serve. I couldn't stop rejoicing. The excitement I felt inside was incredible. The miracle that God did was one of so many. Our needs are always met in God. I'm so very thankful for Him showing us just how amazing He is. Funny thing is, the next time I needed gas I quickly asked again and guess what? Nothing happened. I realized God chooses to do what He wants to do and when He wants to do it. I love His surprises. I believe He was showing both my husband and I a little bit of who He is.

Through the years, I found out something that the Bible is clear on. God loves to give! He moves with our faith! But we have to take the first step! The first step is believing. It amazes me how He loves to show Himself.

It's His good pleasure to give to His children just as it is ours to give to our children. We serve a mighty, big God who wants to lavish and surprise us with all good things.

"Ask and it will be given to you, seek and you find." *(Matthew 7:7, KJV)*

"And if you believe you will receive anything you ask for in prayer." *(Matthew 21:22, KJV)*

"If you, then, though you are evil, know how to give good gifts to your children, how much more will you Father in heaven give good things to those who ask him." *(Matthew 7:11, NIV)*

Chapter

12

Demonic Invasion

The devil showed up in MY house! Stay with me, okay... This story pretty much begins in the middle. Remember how I mentioned that the devil is real. Life in the spirit is very exciting, yet sometimes scary. Let me explain what I'm talking about.

My many spiritual experiences caused friction in my home with my husband. I will be honest on this particular night I'm speaking of I was separated from my husband, so many separations led to our divorce, even after 35 years of marriage. I knew there was a cost when I chose to walk with God, but I couldn't have predicted it would be at the expense of my marriage. But since then I learned that the value of choosing God holds much more worth than what we lose.

"Large crowds were traveling with Jesus, and turning to them he said: If anyone comes to me and does not hate father and mother, wife and children, brothers and sisters—yes, even their own life—such a person cannot be my disciple. And whoever does not carry their cross and follow me cannot be my disciple." (Luke 14:25-27, NIV)

What do you think the term *hate* means in this passage? If we don't hate our family and our own lives, we can't be His disciple? Does God mean that we ought to have hatred for our parents and our spouse, etc.? I would think not.

Jesus goes on to relate an analogy about a man who builds a house without counting the cost and finds that he cannot follow through with what he has set out to do. He leaves the house unfinished because he cannot pay what is required. Jesus is explaining that we must count the cost of discipleship. In other words — in order to be His disciple, we must be willing to give up everything- especially for Him. Therefore, if our parents will not follow Jesus, or even if they disown us for being Christians, we must still choose Jesus over them. This is right in God's eyes. We must love our family members and encourage them, but we are to love God first.

Despite our love for the people closest to us, here is the key: if they don't love Jesus, He must still be our number one priority. We esteem Him more highly than the people we love here on earth and we must love Him more than our own lives. The fact is, we must love Him *so* much that our earthly loves pales in comparison, even to the point of seeming like hate.

No Demons in My House!

Another Wednesday night, I was at church with my children (my husband and I were separated at this time) during the service the pastor suddenly stopped in the middle of his message. He looked directly at me for at least 5-10 seconds. He asked the congregation to stand and join hands to pray. The prayer was in agreement for protection. I knew that prayer was for me. I know it was for everyone, but I especially felt it was for me. I mean, why wouldn't I think that after such a long-concentrated stare. God knew I needed protection because of what was about to happen only hours away.

On the drive back home after that prayer of protection, I was being extremely cautious. The kids were being silly with laughter doing the usual in the back seat, and I wasn't paying much attention to them. I just couldn't get that prayer off my mind.

Home safe, I said underneath my breath. I was exhausted and it was already late. I got the kids tucked in bed with a bunch of love and kisses. Then I went to get ready for bed myself. Just as I was getting comfy and cozy, I heard a noise in my bathroom, it sounded like someone flipping the light switch off and on. Prior to this night, I had experienced some unusual things in the house and discerned that they were demonic spirits. Many times, I had to run evil spirits out of the house and this night was no different. These demons seemed to be territorial, we were in a rented house and hadn't been there long. So, when I had heard the noise in the bathroom, I knew it was an evil spirit. The difference this time was that I had chosen not to be bothered by the enemy. The enemy didn't scare me anymore.

I pulled the covers up and turned over to get comfortable. I was talking to God and boldly stated, "That enemy can't hurt me." Just as I spoke those words to God, the demonic spirit left the bathroom and walked right in front of me. I saw him with the naked eye! Spiritual or naked eyes, it didn't matter. I saw him! Not only did I see him, but the temperature in the room dropped drastically. The presence of this spirit brought a horribly cold and eerie feeling. This evil spirit was tall and had the darkest set of eyes I've ever seen When he walked, his arms swayed with his hands reaching past his knees. It was like a creepy alien or something. As this thing passed me it looked at me and said, "If I can't get to you, then I'm going to get your kids!"

Like a roaring lioness, a boldness came over me like never before! I jumped up and yelled, "Oh no you're not!"

The power of God came on me so strong; I felt His presence on me before my feet even hit the floor! As I went after this evil spirit, he ran like a scared rabbit! I quickly moved into each of my children's bedroom and declared for the angels to watch over them. I laid my hand on their heads and covered them with the blood of Jesus in prayer. Charging after this demonic force, I was quickly in and out of their rooms.

The presence of God was so evident that as I entered the kitchen;

our small pet bird tucked his head up under his wing. Even the bird felt the presence of God! I then commanded the unwanted spirits out of my house! Although I only witnessed one, I felt that there was more than one running to get away. At my command, they fled. *And never returned again!*

The second they all had left the house the neighborhood dogs began barking all at the exact same time!

I had to sit down in awe because of the intense spiritual experience I had just witnessed. All the barking dogs caused the house lights on my street to come on. The neighbors started coming out of their homes to see what all the commotion was. I was overwhelmed with what had just taken place. I chose to stay in God's presence for some time. I kept repeating the words, "God you are so strong. You are so powerful." I had never experienced anything like that before in my life. The power of God that I felt in my body was so prevailing, I can't even describe it! HE'S STRONG AND FIERCE! The enemy didn't see me! He saw God's presence in me and ran away so fast!

The next morning, I was leaving for work and my neighbor came running outside. "Hey, were you home last night?" she asked, with the intent to share her experience. "Did you hear all the dogs barking simultaneously?" A lot of the neighbors had come running outside all at once because the dogs were going crazy! She said, "It was the weirdness thing. None of us could figure out why the dogs were barking at the same time." I just nodded. I didn't say a word about my experience because, just how was I to explain what I knew?

But just as I was getting into my car, I saw that same demon! He went **into** the Great Dane in the yard across the street. *The demon entered into the dog!* I saw his black eyes. I will never forget how dark and demonic they were!

My neighbor's Great Dane was pacing back and forth along the fence looking directly at me! I said to it, "I see you! You can't stay in this neighborhood so get out in Jesus' name!" By God's grace, I never saw the demon again.

At this very moment, God is reminding me of the authority we have in Jesus' name. He has given us authority over the enemy, when we agree with God, His power shows up and He defeats the enemy. The fight is easy as a believer, because God's Spirit lives in us. With that being said, we should *all* stand from a position of *authority, overcoming the evil one!* It is Christ- in-us that the enemy flees from. Our part is knowing who we are and what authority we carry. Since then, I have learned how to bind and loose and the enemy can't invade my territory anymore. I'll share more about binding and loosing later.

I'm so very thankful to have these testimonies. Many readers may believe my stories, and some may not. But the fact remains true, I lived it. With the grace of God, His permission, and His lead, I will speak of the many battles that I have encountered as a testimony of God's faithfulness. As I do, know that All the glory goes to God! He has brought me through so much!

"And they overcame him (the enemy) by the blood of the Lamb, and by the word of their testimony; and they loved not their lives unto the death." (Revelation 12:11)

"But whenever anyone turns to the Lord, the veil is taken away. Now the Lord is the Spirit, and where the Spirit of the Lord is, there is freedom. And we all, who with unveiled faces contemplate the Lord's glory, are being transformed into his image with ever-increasing glory, which comes from the Lord, who is the Spirit." (2 Corinthians 3:17-18)

"For the weapons of our warfare are not of the flesh but have divine power to destroy strongholds." (2 Corinthians 10:4)

Chapter

13

Drunk in the Street

Oh no! Am I seeing what I think I'm seeing? Driving our usual route on the way to church along the narrow, two-lane highway, my daughter and I drove pass the old rundown motel-bar when we witnessed a man sitting on a chair in the middle of the highway! I was scared to death for him. He was either really drunk or had a death wish! Several people stood outside the bar yelling, "Mister! Get out of the street!" and "Hey! You're going to get killed!"

He wasn't responding to their calls at all! I don't know if he had been disoriented or what it was. Maybe it really was a death wish. I was horrified because NO ONE was trying to stop the traffic. The cars were traveling so fast that their speed was too fast to even notice this guy until he was right before them. Everyone was afraid to make a move! I cried out, "Dear Jesus help!" I immediately took my daughter's hand and we began to pray. Not only did we pray, but the thought dropped in my spirit to commission angels so they could stop the traffic and bring the man to safety. As soon as I spoke, the angels were at work. We saw the traffic come to a stop within 5- seconds of that prayer. Both lanes came to a stop! Not one person stepped into the highway, but both lanes came to a stop!

Just then the man stood up, picked up his chair and walked off the highway to safety. I know without a doubt, it was the angels who stopped the traffic and escorted this man out of danger.

Angels are here to assist us! They respond, when you speak as long as it lines up with the will of God. The angels are ministering spirits sent to help us.

As a matter of fact, they are waiting for us to align with God and cooperate with them! Angels are waiting and wanting to go to work on behalf of God's people. I know they're always at work without our knowledge because of their commission from the Lord. But indeed, they go forth when we speak.

Please don't buy into the big lie that we are supposed to not associate with angels. I have called on them many times and I have seen the miracles because of it. The Bible says we are not to worship angels, but we are definitely able to labor with them. The enemy at one point, was one of God's top angels. He has millions cooperating with Him! Think about that for a minute.

Saved by the Grace of God!

While I'm on the subject of angels, I didn't mind my husband going to get together with his buddies, but this time was different. I had a very bad feeling and I pleaded with him not to go out that night. I sincerely felt it was a warning that God was giving me for him.

I remember asking him not to go because I felt like something terrible was going to happen. I got so mad because he wasn't taking me seriously. Out of frustration, I yelled out, "You're on your own. I will not pray for your protection tonight!" I meant it too. I was furious because of how strong the warning was.

Well, he thought about it. He even took a little while making his decision about going, because he sat in his truck for a bit before he left. I could tell he was considering what I said. Unfortunately, he left anyway without listening to me. That evening when I went to bed I said, "Lord, get someone else to pray for him, because I refuse."

Sure enough, God does what He does best! I was later awoken out of my sleep and told to pray NOW! I don't know if I was awoken by an angel or the Lord, but I felt the urgency in the command to pray. The sense to pray was so strong I couldn't delay. While in prayer I became extremely anxious for him. It felt as if he was already dead! The same way I had commissioned the angels to assist my brother, I began to do the same thing for my husband. Not too long after that prayer he came walking through the front door.

I ran to see him asking him what happened because he looked white as a ghost! "I can't talk right now," he said, holding his hands up in surrender as I approached him. I could see the fear all over him. He went into the bedroom and snatched his pillow off the bed then placed it on the floor. "Why the floor?" I questioned. "I just want a solid ground," he responded, still shaken.

The next morning, I went outside and saw that his truck had been wrecked. Can you believe that he ran through a 12-foot fence? Not only did he go through the fence, but he instantly sobered up when his truck came to a sudden stop! It jolted him, and when he looked up, he saw an extremely large oak tree! His truck had stopped only inches from crashing into it! I would be bold enough to say the angels I commissioned that night saved my husband's life.

It's okay to work with the angels. They literally come to earth to help. Read the scriptures and see how the angels work on our behalf.

Angels Protect:

[20] *When he came near the den, he called to Daniel in an anguished voice, "Daniel, servant of the living God, has your God, whom you serve continually, been able to rescue you from the lions?"*

[21] *Daniel answered, "May the king live forever!* [22] *My God sent his angel, and he shut the mouths of the lions. They have not hurt me, because I was found innocent in his sight. Nor have I ever done any wrong before you, Your Majesty."*

[23] *The king was overjoyed and gave orders to lift Daniel out of the den. And when Daniel was lifted from the den, no wound was found on him, because he had trusted in his God. (Daniel 6:20-23, NIV)*

[13] *"Go, find out where he is," the king ordered, "so I can send men and capture him." The report came back: "He is in Dothan."* [14] *Then he*

sent horses and chariots and a strong force there. They went by night and surrounded the city.

¹⁵ When the servant of the man of God got up and went out early the next morning, an army with horses and chariots had surrounded the city. "Oh no, my lord! What shall we do?" the servant asked.

¹⁶ "Don't be afraid," the prophet answered. "Those who are with us are more than those who are with them."

¹⁷ And Elisha prayed, "Open his eyes, Lord, so that he may see." Then the Lord opened the servant's eyes, and he looked and saw the hills full of horses and chariots of fire all around Elisha. (2 Kings 6:13-17, NIV)

Angels Reveal Information:

⁵² Was there ever a prophet your ancestors did not persecute? They even killed those who predicted the coming of the Righteous One. And now you have betrayed and murdered him— ⁵³ you who have received the law that was given through angels but have not obeyed it." (Acts 7:52-53, NIV)

¹¹ Then an angel of the Lord appeared to him, standing at the right side of the altar of incense. ¹² When Zechariah saw him, he was startled and was gripped with fear. ¹³ But the angel said to him: "Do not be afraid, Zechariah; your prayer has been heard. Your wife Elizabeth will bear you a son, and you are to call him John. ¹⁴ He will be a joy and delight to you, and many will rejoice because of his birth, ¹⁵ for he will be great in the sight of the Lord. He is never to take wine or other fermented drink, and he will be filled with the Holy Spirit even before he is born. ¹⁶ He will bring back many of the people of Israel to the Lord their God. ¹⁷ And he will go on before the Lord, in the spirit and power of Elijah, to turn the hearts of the parents to their children and the disobedient to the wisdom of the righteous—to make ready a people prepared for the Lord."

¹⁸ Zechariah asked the angel, "How can I be sure of this? I am an old man and my wife is well along in years."

¹⁹ The angel said to him, "I am Gabriel. I stand in the presence of God, and I have been sent to speak to you and to tell you this good news. ²⁰ And now you will be silent and not able to speak until the day this happens, because you did not believe my words, which will come true at their appointed time." (Luke 1:11-20, NIV)

Angels Guide

20 But after he had considered this, an angel of the Lord appeared to him in a dream and said, "Joseph son of David, do not be afraid to take Mary home as your wife, because what is conceived in her is from the Holy Spirit. 21 She will give birth to a son, and you are to give him the name Jesus, because he will save his people from their sins." (Matthew 1:20-21, NIV)

Philip and the Ethiopian
26 Now an angel of the Lord said to Philip, "Go south to the road—the desert road—that goes down from Jerusalem to Gaza." (Acts 8:26, NIV)

Angels Provide

17 God heard the boy crying, and the angel of God called to Hagar from heaven and said to her, "What is the matter, Hagar? Do not be afraid; God has heard the boy crying as he lies there. 18 Lift the boy up and take him by the hand, for I will make him into a great nation."

19 Then God opened her eyes and she saw a well of water. So, she went and filled the skin with water and gave the boy a drink.

20 God was with the boy as he grew up. He lived in the desert and became an archer. (Genesis 21:17-20, NIV)

5 Then he lay down under the bush and fell asleep.

All at once an angel touched him and said, "Get up and eat." 6 He looked around, and there by his head was some bread baked over hot coals, and a jar of water. He ate and drank and then lay down again.

7 The angel of the Lord came back a second time and touched him and said, "Get up and eat, for the journey is too much for you." (1 Kings 19:5-7, NIV)

Angels Minister

14 Are not all angels ministering spirits sent to serve those who will inherit salvation? (Hebrews 1:14, NIV)

Chapter

14

We're at War!

Headed out to get weekly grocery shopping, I heard God say, "Go left!" I quickly thought, *What? What do you mean go left, Lord?* There were no grocery stores that I knew of in that direction, but I heard the Lord's voice so clearly, so I obeyed.

As I went left, I kept driving and driving, but saw and heard nothing. I drove for quite some time while speaking to God. *"Where are you taking me, Lord? I don't know of a grocery store this way. We've been driving a while now."* Finally, I spotted a small meat market, instinctively I knew this was the place. My first thought was how high the cost of the meat would be, but you see, God didn't send me there for groceries. He had another agenda.

The store was very small and it didn't take long for me to run into Bethany, an old classmate from high school. We weren't even speaking for a full minute before the glory of God showed up. Within a moment of time, Bethany received Christ as her savior. Not only was Bethany affected, but the man behind the meat counter was touched as well!

That day, the glory of the Lord filled that small grocery store. Bethany and I exchanged phone numbers and I left rejoicing. She got saved! The presence of God showed up so fast! His agenda had everything to do with His daughter. You could see the expressions and watchfulness of everyone nearby. I stayed in touch with Bethany and got her plugged into church.

Then, a couple weeks had flown by since our encounter, and one morning while in prayer with two other ladies, I heard God speak. "Call Bethany." Okay Lord, I'll call her right after prayer. *"No, call Bethany now!"* I heard His instructions so clear I proceeded to get up off my knees and went into the kitchen where the phone was. We didn't have cellphones back then, but the house phone was hanging on the wall. I called, when she answered she was in total distress, hysterical and crying very hard. *"I can't take it anymore. I'm ending this now!"* she cried out. I immediately began to bind the devil that was trying to take her life. I yelled, "No! I bind you spirit of suicide and command you to leave her now!" I yelled for the two ladies to cover her in prayer as well. I then took off running and grabbed my purse and keys. I darted out of the house and began to drive towards Bethany's home. The only problem was that I didn't know where she lived.

As I was driving down a two-lane road the most bazaar thing happened. First, I need to mention that the car I was driving was an old Volkswagen with a ton of play in the steering. Plainly put, I had to turn the steering wheel before I could get the car to turn. I was very familiar with driving it and had no problem. Back then, I lived in Southeast Louisiana where the heat and humidity are so bad it slaps everyone in the face when you walk out of the house. No wind or breeze, just hot! That day was no different.

While I drove, I noticed that on the side of the road there were very large sewer barrels placed above ground. Out of nowhere, these barrels began to be thrown in-front of my car causing me swerve to avoid hitting them. I was driving like a maniac. I was swerving left and right to avoid hitting these large objects! I knew there was no wind to cause the barrels to roll in front of my car; so, it was definitely demonic interference! I knew that the enemy wanted to take Bethany out and I was getting in his way. So of course, he was furiously trying to stop me from rescuing her. Knowing this was war, I drove like a wild woman to save her.

I imagined at that moment; God had dispatched His war angels to help me. Not knowing where she lived, I began driving in the direction of the small meat market. I felt that she had to live in that area so that's where I headed. I drove praying in the Spirit, I believed with every fiber in my body that was the only way I could find her. I desperately needed God's help to get me there. I was praying at every turn. I began seeing things such as signs that didn't exist. Supernatural signs showing me the way. Each time I would reach one, I'd get a new direction.

By God's amazing guidance, I sensed when to turn left or right and how long to drive straight. I saw signs like, "This Way with an arrow." Or, I'd hear the soft voice, go straight and then crossover the bridge. I finally reached the area of the meat market and got a heads up from The Holy Spirit to turn into a trailer court. I drove asking for another sign. "Which trailer is hers, Lord? Show me!" I then saw the picture of a tall, long-stem rose in my mind so I kept driving until I found one.

Finally, I pulled up to a trailer where I saw the rose. I quickly jumped out of the car and pulled the six-foot wooden gate open. *Suddenly, a Doberman came charging towards me. I put my hand out, shouted, "Halt!"* The dog stopped in his tracks and I walked past him and approached the door. I bet the reason the dog backed off was because he saw a large angel standing there with me. It didn't concern me whether or not I was at the right house, because I was just following my spiritual instincts. It didn't even cross my mind.

I was truly operating in the spirit, relying completely on The Holy Spirit. One thing is for sure, the dog would have destroyed me if the Spirit of God wasn't in control. I don't even think there was an actual rose in front of her trailer. It was a vision in the spirit realm to guide me to her home.

I got to Bethany in time! She was curled up on her bed weeping. She and I dealt with the drugs around her. She was going to kill herself by the means of overdosing. Bethany's life was saved that day by the Lord and His divine way of showing me directions.

As I was leaving Bethany's home, funny thing, she had to hold her dog back from me. I was no longer walking in the power of the spirit when I left. Once again, I was blown away with the presence and power of God. Talk about being obedient. Me and that dog. Ha! He literally obeyed the command of the Spirit of God by letting me approach the door! Halt! I would have never thought to use that word. It was the spirit of God all the way. What a powerful day. It was a miraculous day and one that I will never forget!

Later, I learned that the enemy was handled the split second that the two prayer partners and I prayed. We took authority in the spirit realm, that's why Bethany was still alive. She was being tormented by a suicidal spirit, but God was watching over her. He was the one who warned me to call Bethany in the first place and then miraculously showed me how to find her home. The entire experience was very dramatic, like a movie. Every time I think of that day, I'm still in awe at His presence and power. I am a co-laborer with Christ.

I stand trembling today at the thought of all the times that I didn't obey God and the results from my disobedience. What happened? What could have been avoided? I pray for the mercy of God to prevail for every moment He spoke and I didn't obey. My prayer is to walk in the spirit and trust Him daily. No longer do I want to question His voice. Mercy, mercy, mercy is my cry.

Chapter

15

Get Off Me Devil!

The title of this chapter was birthed from the words of my little girl. It was a typical school day. The school bus had just pulled up to the bus stop to make its drop off when Linda, my second child who was in elementary school at the time, got off the bus. She looked awful! She walked into the house crying. "Mom, my belly hurts." Her cheeks were very flushed, and I could see that she had a fever so I checked her, she was burning hot. Immediately, I told her, "Go back to the door and open it up then tell the devil – *Get off my body.* and kick him out!"

She was so precious. She opened the door and yelled, **"Get off me devil!" Then she did an air-kick with her foot while holding the door open with her little hand. Her fever broke that instant!** And no more complaints about her stomach pain either. Pretty amazing, huh? The faith of a child is incredible when practiced. At her command, the enemy had no choice but to leave!

Jesus said in Matthew 18, "Truly, I tell you, unless you change and become like little children, you will never enter the kingdom of heaven. Therefore, whoever takes the lowly position of this child is the greatest in the kingdom of heaven." Wow. I wish we'd all believe so easily.

It was shortly after that, Katherine her older sister, got off the middle school bus. She said pretty much the same thing about her stomach and also had a fever. I told her what Linda did, but instead of doing it too, she laughed and made fun of us. "That's stupid," she commented and walked away. But as the story is told, Katherine's stomach virus lingered for a couple of days, which included fever, nausea, and diarrhea. Meanwhile, Linda's fever left completely and instantly. She felt fine the same day with no symptoms and was able to enjoy herself outside playing and eating. She did pretty much whatever she desired. Katherine, not so much.

Allow me to say this: believing or not believing is a choice. We are given dominion over the enemy, but it's up to us to take advantage of it. I don't know why sometimes it works, and sometimes it doesn't, but God has all authority and gives us authority and the free will to believe and receive.

"Submit yourself then to God, resist the devil and he will flee." (James 4:7, KJV)

I personally believe all sickness comes from the enemy. The enemy has nothing on us. Jesus stripped the devil of his rights moments before His resurrection. But, here's the catch to living a free life. We need Jesus in our life to beat the devil. Without Jesus, the devil has every legal right to torment you. It is Jesus he's afraid of, not you. Without Jesus we're doomed.

Submit yourself. That's the key. Then you can resist the devil and he *will* flee! God the Father gave Jesus heaven's authority. Read Matthew 28:18. Then Jesus stripped the devil of his authority in hell. Amazingly enough, **Jesus then goes on to give the believer, the same authority that He received from the Father! We have Jesus' authority!** He gave it to us, but here's the thing: it's up to us to take it and use it. Receive it and believe it. There is power in Jesus' name! We have been given the same authority Jesus had while He was on earth.

Chapter

16

God is that you speaking?

It was the early 80's when I recall clearly hearing God's subtle voice one evening. I was learning to trust and know the sound of it. I had asked The Holy Spirit to teach me His voice beyond a shadow of a doubt and I must say, He did just that. He would speak and have me to do things that were unconventional or out-of-the-box.

One night I was frying chicken for dinner and while standing at the stove, I heard "Go visit your new neighbor. She needs prayer." I thought about it for a moment. How strange would it be for me to walk up to a stranger's door and ask if they needed prayer? I questioned, *"God is that you speaking to me?"*

I felt impressed again. I really wanted to obey what I felt, so I finished cooking, turned off the stove and put the chicken off to the side. I walked two doors down to the new neighbor. She answered the door. I welcomed her to the neighborhood and we proceeded to have small talk. I really wasn't at all sure how to say anything about prayer, but right before I was getting ready to head back home, I built up enough courage and asked if there was something, she might need prayer for.

I admitted to her that I felt led to come and pray for her. Her response was, "YES!" She swung the door open even wider and invited me in. She then hobbled on one leg over to the sofa and put her foot up on the coffee table. She showed me her infected leg with a red streak going up the thigh. I said, "That's a terrible infection. That red streak looks like blood poisoning."

I told her she needed to get to the hospital immediately because the red streak was not anything to ignore. For all we knew it could travel to the heart and become fatal. "I cannot afford to go," she shared. Then boldness came over me. I said, "God instructed me to come and pray for you. Now I know why."

With her permission, I began to pray and lay hands on her leg. I don't remember the prayer and I don't recall feeling or seeing anything happen. All I did was obey what I felt was the voice of God. I left her and I went home to get Neosporin ointment, as if that was going to help. Let me tell you, her wound was *well past* the help of Neosporin.

The next day I was pulling up into the driveway and she came running outside to meet me. She was yelling, "Jennifer! Jennifer! Look!" She then showed me her leg without any sign of infection. The red streak was gone! "After you prayed," she said, "the swelling went down and the wound began to drain. Also, the red streak began to disappear. When I woke up this morning, every sign of the infection was gone!"

The healing was the very first miracle that I had witnessed. The infection and blood poisoning were noticeably there before the prayer. Then after the prayer, they were gone! No other explanation than God's healing power. I ran inside the house, dancing and shouting! I was very excited to see God move. I called my Aunt Therese and shouted, "I got the gift of healing! I got the gift of healing!" She laughed saying, *"You crazy nut! You've got the Holy Ghost and He's got it all!"* That was such a wonderful response.

It *was* the voice of God that first sent me to her house and it *was* His power again that did the healing. There was nothing that I could have done in my own power. His spirit lives inside of me, and it was by His power flowing through me that the healing occurred. I was simply the conduit.

He says, "Lay hands on the sick and they will recover." He heals and sets the captives free. If I would have disobeyed, who knows what would have happened to her?

Blood poisoning travels and kills. I'm sure she would have given in and eventually gone to the hospital, but that prayer saved her life. She didn't need to go to the hospital or receive drugs at that moment. She just needed Jesus! He stepped in and miraculously healed her. I realized that listening to, and obeying, God's voice was what I desired. It benefits not just me, but those around me. It's is exciting and fulling to not only witness, but to be part of someone being healed and to have their faith rise.

Chapter

17

She came out of the Wheelchair

The Lord was answering my prayer for me to hear his voice. I loved how He was teaching me. With His simple request that let me know how to be for sure that it was Him that I was hearing. He has allowed me to witness the miracle of His healing power, simply because I would hear and obey. What a way to learn his voice watching His power heal.

For this second miracle, I was in a fairly large church. I was sitting on the right side of the sanctuary in the middle row of the pews. They were having an altar call at the end of the service. While I was praying for those at the altar, I heard God's gentle voice say, "Go to the lady in the wheelchair." I hadn't even noticed anyone in a wheelchair, I looked around and I saw no one in a wheelchair. I didn't speak out loud, but in my heart, I was asking God to confirm what I felt I heard. *Lord, if this is you, please say it again.* My heart began pounding because seconds later I heard it again. *Lord, I don't mean to be disrespectful, but if this is really you, please say it one more time.* I wanted to be sure. Right then, He repeated the same words, but I still did not know where the lady in the wheelchair was. The moment I obeyed and stepped out of the pew I found myself in the center aisle looking straight at her. I don't even recall walking around to find her. The woman and her son were leaving when she looked at me and stared straight into my eyes! I don't believe she saw me. I truly felt she saw

Jesus in me. She remained in a stare and told her son to remove the pillow from behind her legs. He looked up and saw me and began to stare at my eyes as well. I felt the fire of God in my eyes, much like the way I felt it the night He filled me with His Spirit.

At this point, I didn't know what to say! They were both so fixed on my eyes. I'm confident they saw Jesus in me. My eyes felt so alive.

I was shaken to the core. The Word of God rose up in my spirit and my first words to her were, *"Ma'am, Rise and walk!"* What else should I have said? I mean, it worked for Peter. I stretched out my hand, not even touching her, and while I was stepping backwards, she walked forward. I didn't know what to do except to pray in tongues. She walked! Can you believe it? She walked without anyone's help! The Holy Spirit had an agenda and I got to be a part of it. I went home in a daze that evening. I was in total wonderment. God showed up again, in power!

Before I had arrived home that evening, someone had already told my husband what happened at the church. He was very uneasy about all that was happening with me. When I walked in the door, he was sitting on the lounge chair. He sat up and calmly asked, *"You healed a lady in a wheelchair?"* I threw my hands up and replied, *"I didn't do it. Jesus did!"*

No statement could be more accurate. We have no power in and of ourselves. We can do nothing without Christ. It was the power of The Holy Spirit that raised that lady up from the confinements of her wheelchair. Those that listen and obey are simply the conduit that He works through. Over the years, my experiences become more powerful and profound and I am filled with excitement to see all that God has in store.

Chapter

18

The Power of Our Words

You've heard it said, "Sticks and stones may break my bones, but words can never hurt me." Well, that's a lie that the enemy started a long time ago. Nothing could be further from the truth. Words either build up or tear down! The following verses highlight this very fact.

The tongue has the power of life and death, and those who love it will eat its fruit. (Proverbs 18:21)

A wise man's heart guides his mouth, and his lips promote instruction. (Proverbs 16:23)

Pleasant words are a honeycomb, sweet to the soul and healing to the bones. (Proverbs 16:24)

We must realize our life follows our words. Our thoughts become words therefore; we must realize where our thoughts are coming from. Both God and the enemy put thoughts in our mind. We must learn to discern who we are hearing. Is it God's voice, our own, or the enemy? What we speak and agree with comes alive. We are created in the image of God, remember Here are a few examples of that actually happening.

Leave or Die

One morning, it was a typical warm and sunny day. I remember stepping out the house early before it got too hot, but then again, it was always hot in Southeast Louisiana. I love being outdoors, especially in the early mornings before the heat. I sat down on my lounge chair in my backyard and proceeded to read.

I was sitting close enough to see the garden. When I looked over at the ground, I saw a very large pile of red ants near my vegetables. The ants had built a large mound and they were everywhere! I thought about the authority God had given me so I acted on it. I stretched out my hand toward the ants and commanded them to leave my garden or die.

Later that evening I went outside to water the garden when I realized that all the ants were gone! Not one sign of them was left, they had disappeared! I began to rejoice. My neighbor overheard me. Of course, I spread the good news of what God had done. This may not seem like much, but to me, it shows how the God of the universe cares about even the little things that we care about. This miracle also shows the authority God has given to the believer. That's powerful!

As I am writing this, I'm reminded of being made in the image and likeness of God. We are powerful people when we are filled with the presence of God. When we decree a thing, it's powerful because of the authority that God has given us over all things. The Bible says, "I tell you, you can pray for *anything,* and if you believe that you've received it, it will be yours" (Mark 11:24, KJV).

Oh No, Scales!

When my family and I moved to Atlanta, Georgia from Louisiana, we left much behind. I enjoyed having plants and trees in my home, but I had to leave them all behind when we moved. We simply couldn't fit anything else in our moving truck.

One day while shopping, I noticed some beautiful large indoor trees for sale. I was excited to see them at such a great price that I bought one. A few days later, I was wiping the leaves with a soft towel and noticed scales on the backside of the leaves. A scale is a small flat insect that sucks the sap from plants and robbing them of essential nutrients. This occurs with many houseplants, but how did I not see them before? They were everywhere! Suddenly, I remembered praying and commanding the ants to leave or die, so I prayed and commanded the same of the scales.

Well, that evening at church I was standing at the altar for prayer. I don't remember what prayer I went to the altar for, but the minister gave me a word of knowledge saying, "What you have prayed for has happened." In my heart I knew the minister was referring to the earlier prayer about the scales on the leaves, not the present prayer. I couldn't wait to get home to see the tree. I hurried into the house lifted up the leaves and just as I thought, the scales were gone! Not one trace of the scales was seen. They had all left!

Our prayers are powerful when we believe what we pray. The spoken word has life! Unfortunately, oftentimes we don't even realize it. Our spoken word creates like God's spoken word. We are created in His image and likeness. Words are extremely important; they literally bring life or death.

The Hidden House

Around this same time, I regularly would drive past a newly built house which was hidden behind a huge tree. Each time I passed that house I practically cursed that tree, not with bad language, but with my words. Comments like, "That tree is in the way of that cute little house and needs to be cut down." I even verbally declared that it would be removed. I felt the tree wasn't very pretty and was an eyesore to everyone who looked at it. I believed it really needed to be removed. After all, you couldn't see the pretty little house that was hidden behind it.

One day as I was driving past the house with my cousin who

lived just around the corner from that home, I yelled, "Yay! They're cutting the tree down and it's about time!"

"Oh no," my cousin said, "Why are you rejoicing? They built that house there because of that tree. The home owners wanted the shade that the tree provided."

My heart sank, I felt terrible. I'm not saying that the tree died because of my spoken words, but what if? Honestly, it felt like I caused it. Only God really knows if I did. It may be presumptuous of me to think that, but, what if? That incident made me really think about how powerful our words are. After all, we are created in the image and likeness of God. If He spoke things into existence, then we have the authority to speak just like He did.

"Therefore, I tell you, whatever you ask for in prayer, believe that you have received it, and it will be yours." (Mark 11:24, NIV)

Chapter

19

Katherine's Ears
Followed by Deception

The challenge of ending my daughter's multitude of ear infections made me relentless. For a while, I feared that she was in danger of losing her hearing. The ear problems started when she was six weeks old. By the age of 11, she had experienced four surgeries which included tubes in her ears for drainage.

The infections would get so bad that it actually ate a hole in her ear drum, which caused them to bleed. Her body became so immune to the antibiotics that it no longer was getting rid of the infections. When her ear drum started to bleed, I became very scared. I felt the guilt of it too! I had asked God numerous times to heal her ears and nothing happened. During a church message, I had heard a line that really stuck with me. The minister said that it was okay for us to remind God of His Word. So that same day, I came home and went into my prayer closet to do just that (By the way, I would literally go into my bedroom closet to pray. I found it to be a very quiet and undisturbed place). My children knew not to bother me if the closet light was on and the door was closed.

Anyway, I was in the closet praying and I reminded God of His Word from Matthew 21:22 that says, "And all things, whatsoever ye shall ask in prayer, believing, ye shall receive." So boldly, I prayed and said, "God your Word says to ask, believe, and receive. I have asked, I *do* believe and still haven't received. Why haven't you performed?" At that moment, I heard him say, "Because she doesn't believe."

Immediately, I thanked Him. I got up and went straight to Katherine. I told her that I was in prayer talking to God and I heard Him give me a response. I pleaded with her to open her heart and simply take Him at His word. She agreed, so when went to church and had believers agree with us. Jesus said in Mark 16:18 that believers would lay hands on the sick and the sick would recover. So that's exactly what we did.

In Katherine's case, all those years, I simply believed on her behalf. I was the one expecting to see God move the entire time because Scripture says for us to ask, believe, and we will receive. Katherine's belief opened the pathway to receive.

I took Katherine back to the doctor and he confirmed her healing, he said, "The scar tissue was still there, but she no longer had a hole in her ear drum and the infection was gone."

Deception Came Quick

A few days later, Katherine came up the hallway pulling her finger out of her ear. She said, "Mom look!" There was blood on her finger tip. Immediately, the Holy Spirit let me know it was a trick of the enemy. I said, "Don't believe it. That blood is a lie! You have been healed. The enemy wants you to believe that you weren't. Go wash up and continue to thank God for healing you." She never had another issue with her ears.

God is a miracle worker when it comes to healing. His grace, mercy and forgiveness endure forever.

SADLY, I believe part of the reason why Katherine suffered with her inner ear infections was because I had been a cigarette smoker for many years.

Statistics show that cigarette smoke causes the ears to become infected. She could have lost her hearing because of my bad habit. I thank God that His mercy prevailed. This is why we pray!

And they overcame him (the enemy) by the blood of the Lamb and by the word of their testimony; and they loved not their lives unto the death. (Revelation 12:11)

But whenever anyone turns to the Lord, the veil is taken away. Now the Lord is the Spirit, and where the Spirit of the Lord is, there is freedom. And we all, who with unveiled faces contemplate the Lord's glory, are being transformed into his image with ever-increasing glory, which comes from the Lord, who is the Spirit. (2 Cor. 3:17-18)

For the weapons of our warfare are not of the flesh but have divine power to destroy strongholds. (2 Cor. 10:4)

Chapter

20

Healed in the Grocery Store

One day while shopping for groceries, I ran into an old neighbor who used to live next door to me. We were having small talk when she shared with me that she was going for surgery in the morning. I felt prompted by the Lord to pray for her to be healed, but I really didn't want to. However, I felt the nudge to pray so I obeyed. I asked if she believed in healing and thankfully, she was receptive. So, I began to pray.

One thing I know is that when God says to do something, you do it. No questions asked. The results are up to Him. The surgeons were going to work on a main nerve and several muscles in my neighbor's leg and the recovery would require complete bed rest for at least six weeks afterward. As I began to pray, I bent down and laid hands on her leg. I then told her to ask the doctor in the morning to re-examine and affirm if surgery was needed.

During the prayer, I honestly felt Jesus had instantly healed her condition through faith. I gave her my business card and asked her to let me know what the doctor had said. By the end of the week, I still had not heard from her.

That Sunday, my husband came home from playing golf and said he ran into her husband at the range. He had yelled out to my husband, "Dude, your wife healed my wife at the grocery store." My wife said, her leg felt different even while walking to the car!"

Of course, it was not me that healed her. It was the power of God that healed her.

Later that afternoon she and her husband were knocking at the front door. I opened and yelled with excitement! I asked, "Why didn't you call me?!" She pulled the business card from her purse and tossed it to me. "Who is this?" I said. *Oh no!* I had given her someone else's business card!

In that moment, we had a good laugh. As she told me about the morning of her operation, she mentioned how she wished she would have taken my advice and requested an examination prior to her surgery, but unfortunately, she didn't. Upon making the surgical incision, the doctors discovered that her leg was now completely healthy! She was cut open unnecessarily since she had already healed!

Come on, Jesus! The surgery and the scar could have been avoided. Not to mention the expense. At any rate, Jesus healed not only her leg but He increased her faith, as well as her husband's! Every time she looks at her leg, her scar is a constant reminder of God's goodness.

Chapter

21

Three Months to Live

I lived in a beautiful neighborhood and nearly every day I would wake up about 6 a.m. to spend time with God, walk and watch the sunrise. I found that walking and talking with God time so fulfilling. I absolutely loved how I felt when we communicated during that period.

One morning, I woke up earlier than usual. The time on the clock was around 4:30 a.m. and I just couldn't go back to sleep. I figured, *hey… why not just go for an early morning walk.* So, I did. While walking my neighborhood, I prayed for each home as I strolled passed it. As I approached my friend Miranda's house, I sensed the presence of God moving very strong. As a matter of fact, while I was praying, I had to stop walking because I felt a heavy sense of His spirit. It was so strong that I couldn't walk any further.

I doubled over and wept as I prayed for her. This prayer of intercession lasted for some time. Finally, I composed myself, as I lightly tapped on her front door with hopes that she just might be awake. I do recall her telling me once that she was usually up by 5 a.m., I hoped she would hear me knock. Still no answer, as I continued to knock very lightly. I really wanted to check on her. I felt the prayer was for the battle of her soul. I tried calling her several times later that day and still was unable to reach her.

A few days later Miranda called me and shared that she had been diagnosed with stage four cervical cancer and lung cancer! What?

WOW a double whammy! She was given only a few months to live. When I received the horrible news, I had peace knowing that from the way I felt The Holy Spirit move on me, she would *live and not die*. I shared with Miranda how the spirit of God had me intercede for her that early morning. I mentioned that we needed to stand together believing and declaring God's word for total healing. And with full hope and faith in God, we did just that. We literally took God at His Word.

Weeks went by and Miranda continued to prevail. She stood strong throughout the fourth stage. Her confidence remained in God that He would remove every trace of that horrible devil that was trying to take her life. I recall one night when I was headed to church, I realized that God was prompting me to not go to the building, but instead to go and *be* the church.

You see, as believers in Jesus, we are the church. We don't just sit in a building that has four walls. We are the temple of God and Miranda's temple was being invaded by an unwanted and unwelcomed devil (or should I say devils). When the spirit of God prompted me to go run them off, I went. Both Miranda and I ran the devil off!

> *"And these signs will accompany those who believe: In my name they will drive out demons; they will speak in new tongues; they will pick up snakes with their hands; and when they drink deadly poison, it will not hurt them at all; they will place their hands on sick people, and they will get well."*
> *(Mark 16:17-18) NIV*

Miranda's healing began the moment she asked God to heal her body and the manifestation (proof) came afterwards. The fact is, God is true to His Word and He delivers His people from every trial and situation, even if heaven is the destination of delivery.

The Bible tells us, *"Many are the afflictions of the righteous, but the Lord delivers him from them all (Psalms 34:19) NIV*

For several months, Miranda endured the trial of her life while standing and believing that God's Word was and would always be true. She didn't waver, but believed in spite of losing her hair. She pressed through much pain and suffering. It was the roughest time of her life and she remained steadfast by fighting the good fight of faith.

This is a decade old story and I always enjoy retelling it. Today, my friend is still alive and 100% free from those cancerous demons. Miranda has since remained in the faith with a smile, staring down her adversary, confidently knowing that her God is Greater! Without a doubt, the Lord is faithful to heal and deliver. Yes, I said deliver!

I believe that cancer was an attack straight from the enemy of our souls. When she and I talk, we regularly bring up her battle and how merciful God was. Miranda once shared with me how much she appreciates life now and how grateful she is that God saved her. She speaks of how He saved her soul more than her body. In her own words, she said she would live through it again if it meant getting herself right with God. When she called out to heaven in despair, He answered her prayer. She said that she had the most intimate encounters with Him during the darkest hours of her life. There is no person or thing that could ever take God's place.

Sadly though, the unexpected happened. There is a tragedy in this story as well. Miranda's mother, a beautiful, strong believer was in much pain watching her daughter suffer the way she was. While Miranda's battle was taking place, her mother said a prayer that I believe didn't need to be said. Her prayer was, "God please take it off of her and put it on me."

I personally believe that God didn't put that the disease on Miranda; the enemy did. Therefore, when her mom asked for it to be transferred, the enemy didn't hesitate to enter that opened door. Unfortunately, her mom died three months later. It was in those three months that Miranda experienced to a greater extent just how much her mother loved her.

I don't believe God wanted her mother to leave the earth then, but who's to say? All I know is that He does give us all a free will.

It's just tragic that she said those specific words to help her daughter through that rough time. But then again, a lot of parents have directed similar words to heaven concerning their precious children too when sickness or disease is present. One thing is for sure, the love Miranda's mom had for her daughter prevailed none the less.

On a more positive note, Miranda's mom went to be with her Savior. Scripture tells us, *"To be absent from the body is to be present with the Lord."* When you are one of God's children, by accepting Jesus as Lord and Savior, your soul and spirit live on forever in heaven with God. You win no matter what! When you don't accept Him, you lose no matter what. Your soul and spirit will still live on forever, but it won't be in heaven. This may be a bold statement for some, but simply put, if you are not serving Jesus, then you are serving the devil.

The reason why I mentioned Miranda's mom was because I felt it is necessary that we realize this spiritual war we are all in is real. The enemy hates mankind and wants to destroy our inner-self every opportunity he gets.

"For our struggle is not against flesh and blood, but against the rulers, against the authorities, against the powers of this dark world and against the spiritual forces of evil in the heavenly realms." (Eph. 6:12, NIV)

"The thief comes only to steal and kill and destroy; I have come that they may have life, and have it to the full." (John 10:10, KJV)

Chapter

22

Divorced brought poverty!

My husband and I were fortunate to share our new large home, which turned out to be a blessing. Our grown children had families of their own, but due to different financial issues, they all returned to the nest. Our house was filled with our children and grandchildren. While the circumstances that brought us all together were difficult, the end result of all being together warmed my heart.

At this time, we had been married for 35 years. We had stayed together longer than we should have, but you always hold out hope that things will improve. I was reluctant to divorce sooner not wanting to put my children in poverty. The marriage wasn't healthy and it was time we decided to divorce.

Due to the living situation and the cost of supporting the large household, I made the decision to be the one to leave. I felt it was best and most selfless choice I could make. Since the children were residing there, I found myself not fighting for possessions to take with me as I started my new life. In hindsight, it was quite foolish. I declined to seek out an attorney's advice or guidance. Though I was rightfully entitled to some monetary compensation. I chose the quickest route to peace. Since I chose to make this walk alone, I ended up in desperate financial shape. Because everyone functioned so well, I didn't want to disrupt the flow of the home. Therefore, I decided to be the one to leave. My husband wouldn't have ever agreed to leave, so for me to leave was 100% my choice, and what I thought was the best choice for everyone.

I was in the real-estate industry and the market crashed. My savings were quickly exhausted and property wasn't selling. My ex-husband said that he would provide some assistance to me, but that never materialized. The struggle was exhausting. I was in bad shape and I financially and told my children that I would be moving back to my hometown in Louisiana in hope of some emotional support from my family. It was extremely hard on me since all my children were living with my X-husband in our new home. I couldn't even visit my children or grandchildren at will.

When discussing my moving back to Louisiana, my daughter Linda quickly said, "No, Mom! We will find a new place to live so that you can live with us." And that was the direction we took. I was extremely thankful and appreciative of Linda's love and support. My youngest daughter was in college and unable to help.

We had a plan, however, at the same time my dignity and dreams were shattered. I fought hard to remain happy in the face of poverty. I had made a bad decision not protecting myself financially and I had to live with the consequences.

A couple of years after we had settled into our new living arrangement, my girls and their children made plans for us all to go roller skating together. I re-arranged my schedule so that I would be available. I was thrilled at the thought of being surrounded by them all for the afternoon. It wasn't very frequent that I got to see Katherine's children since her death.

One problem my X-husband called and changed the plans. He asked them all to go to his farm and ride horses instead of roller skating. Of course, I wasn't included in the updated plans.

My heart was broken, my feelings were hurt and an argument soon broke-out between me and my daughters. This was my moment of realization. It was time to go make a fresh start, completely on my own again.

Chapter

23

Move!

I was done. I had reached my limit. A friend had mentioned a church that was having a New Year's Eve service so I decided to go alone. I literally knew no one there. I needed for Jesus to take the wheel and help me into the New Year. Alone in the sanctuary I had never attended, surrounded by total strangers, I felt that this was where I was supposed to be. During the service, the guest speaker made a unique statement, "There is a lady here with us tonight. Your children just broke your heart, but the Lord wants to heal you."

I lifted my hand so fast and went forward for prayer. At the altar, the Lord touched my heartache and it disappeared instantly! I cried all the way home, as I had been reminded just how very good God is.

The following morning, a friend and I attended our own church service. After lunch we went to her apartment. It was such a warm and inviting complex, I knew instantly that this is where I wanted to make my new home. Unfortunately, I was drawing unemployment and had filed bankruptcy the previous summer. There was no way I could quality for the lease.

On the way home I was feeling very impressed to apply for the apartment. Turning back into my daughter's subdivision where I was still living, I asked God, "Lord, could I actually be able to move into that nice apartment?" At the exact moment, a car passed me with a front license plate that read, MOVE! I started laughing, knowing that God was providing direction.

Unfortunately, my biggest problem was my income. My doubts were so loud back then. My mind kept telling me that I couldn't qualify to live in that apartment complex due to my money situation. To be able to prove a money flow of $3,000 or more per month was a joke, because my unemployment didn't pay squat. To make matters worse, it had been more than a year since my divorce, and I still needed to remove my name from the mortgage. The next day, I headed over to the apartment complex to speak with the leasing agent about availability and additional information. We discussed things like how many bedrooms, what floor, and how soon? I let her know all my preferences and said, "March first. Two bedrooms. And I'd really like the bottom level."

While I filled out the application, she informed me that she only had a suite available on the 3rd floor. She handed me the keys to go check out the apartment and while I did, she ran my credit and checked on my finances. Walking up those stairs I knew that it wasn't going to be an easy thing to do every day, but it didn't matter. I wanted my own place. Once I stepped through the front door, I looked around and talked with God.

"Lord, you know I don't like the carpet. And I would really enjoy the first floor. But if this is where you want me, then this is where I'll go." As we were talking, I heard in my spirit, *you'll be moving February first.*

Re-entering the manager's office, she looked up at me with a smile. She said, "I have good news for you. The application process went well. And I just received notice that a bottom level unit will soon be available. They are removing the existing carpet and replacing it with what looks like wood floor, would that work? The only problem is this: you will need to sign a lease for the first of February instead of the first of March.

"Wow. Okay. sounds good. By the way, how was my credit?" I asked, with a smile of my own.

"It all checked out fine," she replied. "No deposit needed and your income qualifies." At that moment, I thought to myself, *whose credit and bank account did she look at? Couldn't have been mine.* I had experienced a bankruptcy 8 months earlier and was still on unemployment! I was convinced though… Once God told me to move, I gave it a shot. It was a miracle and more miracles kept coming.

When I moved into the apartment complex on the first day of February, I remember unpacking with very little furniture. I had mostly kitchen stuff in my possession and some décor. I had a bed, a dresser, a washer, and a dryer. my TV and 2 lawn chairs. Oh, let's not forget my iron and ironing board. I wanted to get settled in, but I had a commitment with the church the same day. I would've felt terrible if I reneged on my word so I decided to put my stuff aside and go serve the Lord as promised.

My Roommate

The church event was a 3-day conference. On the first day, a lady who we will call Debbie came to the door looking pretty rough. She had been homeless and had been gang affiliated in Florida for some time. She stated that it was a friend of hers that had purchased a plane ticket and put her up in a hotel right up the street from the conference. The agreement was that she had to attend the conference. When I saw her, I greeted her but she was very stand-offish and noticeably protected herself.

On the second day of the conference, I felt led to take her home and offer her a place to live. Definitely not my choice.

Truth be told, I fought the thought of it for several reasons, but the direction to take her in remained. I had nothing to offer her such as a soft bed or a comfy sofa to sleep on. I don't know what I was thinking. I didn't even know how I was going to pay my monthly bills. All I know was that it was The Holy Spirit impressing me to give her a place to live. As the thoughts continued to re-occur, I walked to the back of the church and prayed. I kept feeling the pull within my spirit to offer her a place to stay. So, I continued to pray a little while longer and then finally I heard God speak. He said, "Paul and Debbie are in the dining area go speak with them."

When the Lord says to do something, you just do it. He always has a good reason. I went as I was told. While in the middle of my conversation with them, I looked at Debbie. As direct as I could've been, I said, "You're coming home with me." It just flew right out of my mouth! What? What did I just say? I couldn't believe what I was getting myself into.

After the conference, while driving home, I thought, *what have I just done?* The next morning, my girlfriend called in a panic. Jennifer, what are you doing?" She asked concerning my offer to welcome a complete stranger into my new apartment. "She could be carrying drugs, girl. She's a gang member!" I knew my friend's heart just wanted the best for me and she was simply doing what friends do for each other, but I also knew she wasn't in line with the voice of God at that moment.

I shook my head lightly and said, "Hey, I really need to go and pray. I'll let you know how it all turns out." She agreed to let me go. When we hung up, I got off the phone and talked to the Lord some more. This was a huge decision. I prayed, asking God to confirm what I was doing. I turned on the TV and surprisingly, the first thing that came on was a song.

The lyrics went like this:

That's the way I planned it.
That's the way I want it to be.

Then the next song's lyrics were heard:

He's going to take you higher.

I believed right then that I was hearing God's voice again. I began to cry, "Lord, I want a husband, not a grown woman. Please give me another word."

He said, "Get the room ready." I turned off the TV without hesitating and went into the secondary bedroom. I began to empty a few boxes at the same time I cried and prayed. "Lord, please can I have another word?" He spoke, *"Sure, turn on the TV."*

I returned to the living room and flipped the TV back on. Can you believe it? The same two songs came on! It was His plan and I needed to obey.

On that Sunday evening, Debbie came home with me and stayed for two months. Over that time span she received deliverance and freedom in her heart. By God's wonderful grace, she became a very powerful vessel of God. It's been years now since this story has taken place and we honestly have not been in touch. However, I must say, the apartment turned out to be a real blessing for myself and many others who have stayed there over time.

I remember another instance of a second young lady who I had offered the bedroom. She on the other hand, ended up staying there a much longer time. When she did leave, I felt led not to fill the space with another roommate, but to create a stream of income by renting the room through Air B&B. The moment I did that, people from different states and countries came to stay with me. Some of them stayed for a day or so, while others stayed for months. I loved meeting people from other countries. During that season, my world became very interesting. Numerous people got saved through staying in my little, two-bedroom apartment. I have met and became friends with many people in that little apartment. My life has never been the same since then.

Thinking back on those days, God taught me so much. He allowed me to learn through the good, and even difficult, times in that apartment. I saw Him fill that apartment with love and even material things. Remember how I started out lacking much furniture. Well, because I needed a sofa, I asked for one. The next week, my neighbor said she was receiving a new sofa and offered me her used one. So of course, I accepted.

Debbie called me one day saying, "There are some people wanting to bring in a sofa. What do you want me to do?" I answered her, "Let them in."

When I arrived to the apartment, I thanked God of course, but I also laughed. After I saw it, I swiftly found myself heading to the store to see if I could buy a sofa cover because boy it was ugly. It wasn't very comfortable either. It was then that I realized I should've used the word "New" when I asked God for the furniture. I wasn't specific enough. I felt like the Lord was teaching me something in that experience.

So, at my next opportunity, what do you think I did? The next piece of furniture I needed was a dining room table. Therefore, I stood in the empty dining room area and requested a *new* dining table. It was only days later that I received a phone call from a local ministry.

"Hi, there. Are you still looking for a dining table?" the gentleman from a benevolence ministry asked.

"Yes," I replied with excitement in my voice.

"Well, we just received one in a box. It's brand new. You'll need to put it together though. Will that be okay?"

I just laughed. "Yes. That's fine. When can I pick it up?"

Once I picked it up, I brought it to the apartment. Thankfully a friend was available to help me put it together. In the middle of my dancing and rejoicing, I stopped and looked into the living room at the old sofa. "Lord, I'm going to give this old sofa away to someone else who needs it. I would like to ask for a *new* sofa!"

The same day, I placed an ad stating FREE SOFA. Can you believe it? That old thing was picked up before the night had ended! The same week, I received a phone call from my daughter. Hi, "Mom, do you remember Charlie, the guy in my neighborhood. You listed his house. Well, he bought a brand-new sofa, but now needs to move. He is not taking it with him. You should give him a call."

I called Charlie the same day but he said he had already sold it and was just waiting on the guy to pick it up. When I hung up the phone, I prayed, "Lord if the other guy does not need the sofa as bad as I do, please allow me to get it."

Two days later, Charlie called me. And guess what? I got a brand-new leather reclining sofa for only $500.00. That was less than half the original cost. I have so many stories just like that. I'm thankful to be writing this particular story because you and I both need the reminder of how God enjoys honoring our prayers. He loves lavishing His kids with what we need and often times want.

Delight thyself in the Lord, and he shall give thee the desires of your heart. *(Psalm 37:4, KJV)*

Chapter

24

"A Parent's Nightmare"

As the doctor approached us in the waiting room, he was struggling to find the words to say and the way to get them out. "Your daughter went into cardiac arrest. We did everything we could do," he stammered. I suppose I knew what he meant the moment I saw the expression on his face as he walked into the room. However, my heart couldn't quite grasp the magnitude of the situation. I interrupted him, *"Doctor, please* just tell us how she is at this very moment."* By the look on his face I knew what he was about to say. He very compassionately spoke the worst words a parent could hear. *"She passed."*

My heart stopped! The room was spinning. I couldn't believe my ears. My husband shouted, *"What?!"* Unable to breathe or even think, I asked if we could see her. At that moment, it was my intention to try and raise her from the dead. I literally tried to do just that, over and over. Brokenhearted, I prayed and prayed. My heart couldn't receive what I was witnessing. I didn't want it to be so! Finally, I had accepted the fact that she wouldn't even consider coming back after being in the total presence of God.

As I reflected upon the recent events, I realized that the signs were there that she was ready to go home and be out of pain. I recall gazing at her the night before and sensing the peace that enveloped her. In hindsight, I know that she must have already been visiting with Jesus in order to embrace that level of peacefulness under those circumstances.

Our nightmare began the day she was admitted into the hospital. There it was, five days after the dreadful phone call my beautiful daughter had passed and I was crushed, numb and overwhelmed all at once. What was I going to do without my precious Katherine? Her laughter wasn't going to be heard anymore and not being able to see her beautiful smile. I couldn't bare the thought.

She left all the pain and suffering and was now and she is in a glorified state. If she didn't know Jesus, I would have lost it for sure. I had a peace that was coming from the Spirit of God within me. Jesus literally held me together. It was many hours later before we left the hospital. It took much longer for the reality to settle in that I would never see her again. It was the worst feeling in the world. My heart ached, yet I was numb.

I was driving home from the hospital; *I couldn't believe my eyes.* The clouds open up and I saw Katherine! She was twirling and twirling, and then came to an abrupt stop. She cupped her hands to her mouth and shouted, *"Mom, it's better than you could imagine!"* Both shocked and excited I started screaming, "OH, my baby! I was trying to say what I was witnessing to my youngest daughter Lynn, and her boyfriend who were riding with me. *Lynn began to yell, "shut up, shut up, mom there is nothing good about this!"* Her response was totally understandable. Neither of them was able to see the vision.

What peace flooded my soul at the very moment I saw her. It was so dear to me. How amazing it was to see my precious daughter dancing in the clouds the day she went home! What a glorious sight that will **never** be forgotten. That vision will remain etched in my heart and mind forever. I am so thankful for that moment. God is so kind!

It was about a week after Katherine's death, I was sitting in bed reading my Bible. The TV was on but it was muted. It seemed as if the words were coming off the page. I felt the presence of God in the room. I then glanced up and I saw words scrolling across the TV screen that had nothing to do with the program airing. The words read:

Thank you ...... I love you ......

I lost it! I couldn't see anything else because my eyes were filled with tears. I knew it was a message from my precious daughter. Those words were desperately needed. They brought closure to my heart regarding some things that had been left unsaid. God will sometimes allow our departed loved ones to send us messages for our healing and for closure. Please understand that I was not having a conversation with the dead, but simply reading the message that was brought to me. Necromancy is forbidden in the scriptures. It's evil in God's sight.

Chapter

25

The Enemy Struck Again

Life is not always easy, in fact, it's downright hard. I had lost my 25-year-old child. My 35-year marriage ended. Then to add to my injury my trifecta was completed with the passing of my 12-year-old granddaughter.

Diane was Katherine's youngest child, who was two months old when her mother passed away. Twelve years after that tragedy, this sweet child left us after being diagnosed with the same disease as her mother. Diane woke up went to tell dad she wasn't feeling well, she passed out in her dad's arms and went into a coma and didn't wake up.

It was Halloween when the enemy struck this time*!*

After I received the call that my grandbaby had been rushed to the hospital and was now in a coma, I felt everything in me saying that this was a battle with the enemy.

After praying, I worshipped God to keep my mind clear. I left the hospital chapel and returned to Diane's side. While in stride, I received a text from an unknown caller which was in large font. I've never seen that size font on a text message before. The message had a picture of two pumpkins, followed by "HAPPY HALLOWEEN, JENNIFER!" I knew it as the enemy.

I cried out, "You haven't won anything!" I had a horrible feeling as I ran the rest of the way to her room praying all the way.

Losing my daughter was hard enough, but losing her baby from the same disease 12 years later was simply tragic. My heart was broken and our entire family was devastated. We lost the battle for her life to remain here on earth that night but we haven't lost the war! I believe 100% that my daughter and granddaughter are at home in Heaven.

It's the devil's plan to keep you from making it to heaven. He failed with my children. Their lives were shortened here on earth but not lost!

I know that they are both rejoicing and enjoying life to the fullest. I sometimes wonder what they're doing. Dancing, singing, what's their vocation? I know Katherine is no longer working as a R.T. in a hospital. There is no sickness or sorrow in heaven. She was also a beautiful singer. I know she's using her beautiful singing gift! Diane was so young; she didn't even have a chance to decide what she would be doing. I just wonder.

Diane's burial plot was with her mother's. Driving to the service was all too familiar and the pain was doubled. I felt like I was re-living Katherine's death as well.

My friend Jeff and I were driving to the funeral service and I wasn't doing so well. Jeff suggested that we look to God and worship. The moment we began to worship peace came and I received a vision of Katherine and Diane! Katherine was holding a basket of rose petals and tossing them into the air. When Diane began blowing on them, they transformed into butterflies. What a beautiful sight. It was a reminder of their freedom!

Another Vision. Shortly after Diane's death, I was alone in my living room feeling empty with so much loss. Suddenly, Katherine showed up in front of me with Diane standing next to her. It was such a glorious sight to see them together!

Diane waved saying, "Hey Nana!" Then using both hands, Katherine blew a kiss saying, "We love you mom." It makes me cry just to think about that moment. I remember it so clearly and it still brings me joy. What a sight! My heart became full at that moment.

As an encouragement to someone who may need to hear this, our loved ones are alive and will always remain alive. They are no longer in a body (earth suit). They have no limitations anymore.

Word of caution: We are not to communicate with the deceased, nor are we to worship them. I was simply given a glimpse of them which brought me comfort.

Chapter

26

With Jesus you win

I have learned that trials in life can either strengthen us or destroy us. Our battle with disease came straight from the enemy and struck my family twice!

It felt as though the devil was shoving it all in my face. If you don't already know, allow me to share that Halloween is a Satanic Holiday and the world is oblivious to it!

Society makes it a fun day, but in reality, satanic orders are driven very high leading up to that particular day on the calendar every year. Just like we pray to God, the satanic worshippers are praying too. They feed on the power and money the enemy gives them when they serve him. Satanists serve Satan as their god and give their allegiance to him. The darkness and hatred of the devil literally becomes a part of the individual for greed and power.

Once again, I must add, the devil is real and he is very destructive. For much of my life I second guessed this fact, but I was reminded of my ignorance many years ago on Halloween when my daughter Katherine was about three. At that time, I had not been taught the truth about Halloween. This was prior to my surrender to Jesus. Anyway, my girlfriend and I made costumes for our girls and they were both dressed up as pumpkins. We stuffed the costumes with balloons and made them big and round. They looked adorable! But like I said, in my ignorance and with the enemy not playing games, he threw his fiery arrow at me many years later. You may say it's nothing, or perhaps it's a coincidence, but I say it was deliberate! It was Halloween Night that I received the two pumpkin pictures on my phone saying, "Happy Halloween Jennifer!"

My advice is this: don't even play with the devil's, especially on the most ungodly night of the year. Halloween is no game! In the past, I wouldn't have written this because I don't want to cause fear, but parents, you need to know this. *This is not fear talking. It's precaution!* The only way anyone can win against the enemy is to be on Jesus' team. It's our responsibility to protect our children. The absolute best thing you can do is cover your children with the blood of Jesus.

It is a parent's role to introduce their children to Jesus. He is the One we must learn from concerning *who* we are and *how* to fight. The perfect age for accountability is around 11 or 12, perhaps even younger for some, but please be sure to receive Jesus for yourself, and share Jesus with your children. It's so important to teach our children about the Savior of the world. Teach them their identity in Christ early. Salvation is a must in order to prevail against the enemy of our soul. We are spiritually covered by the blood of Jesus. Without His blood-covering we are left uncovered and wide open for destruction.

I love what Ephesians 6:10–17 says. Not only is the blood of Jesus our first layer of covering, but we have a second layer which is the full armor of God! It equips us to do battle and be victorious!

---

10 Finally, be strong in the Lord and in his mighty power. 11 Put on the full armor of God, so that you can take your stand against the devil's schemes. 12 For our struggle is not against flesh and blood, but against the rulers, against the authorities, against the powers of this dark world and against the spiritual forces of evil in the heavenly realms. 13 Therefore put on the full armor of God, so that when the day of evil comes, you may be able to stand your ground, and after you have done everything, to stand. 14 Stand firm

then, with the belt of truth buckled around your waist, with
the breastplate of righteousness in place, 15 and with your
feet fitted with the readiness that comes from the gospel of
peace. 16 In addition the shield of faith, with which you can
extinguish all the flaming arrows of the evil one. 17 Take
the helmet of salvation and the sword of the Spirit, which is
the word of God. (Ephesians 6:10-17) NIV

The word of God teaches us that our battle is not against flesh and blood, but against principalities. Learning to trust God took some time for me and honestly it wasn't the easiest thing to do. With all the let downs that have occurred in life, I had two decisions to make. I could have either learned to trust God more or become bitter and blame Him. A lot of people think God is the bad guy, the one who allows so much pain to happen. They question why He didn't do this or that?

He's saying to us, I gave you my authority to take dominion over the earth. Pick up your armor, use it, and go forth. We need to take an offensive position with the enemy. The battle would be easy if we just incline our ear to the brilliant one Jesus. He will direct our path and show us who, what, when and where. The closer I become to The Holy Spirit the more information and instruction I'm given to win this war.

I know we have all experienced some type of extremely painful situations before; some worse than others. For myself, I'm still growing and learning to trust God when I go through those dark valleys. But He has proven Himself faithful so many times that even when I feel my world is falling apart around me, I remind myself of His character. As I distinguish His voice from all the others and walk in obedience, my inner peace and joy comes in great measure.

Recently I've learned to love God with no restraints because He first loved me that way. By getting to know Him, I began to discover who and what I am to Him. I personally don't think we can truly love God until we get to know Him. We must allow Him to teach us how to love ourselves. Throughout this process of love, we begin to love others too.

Over the years, I have learned that Satan and his demons hate God and us. When God withdraws Himself from those who disobey Him, it is because the devil is tied to our disobedience. Yet we must realize obedience *is* our key to God's blessings. It is time to remove the doubt in our mind and trust Him at His Word in our hearts. When my heart gets heavy at times, I have to remember to press on. I realize I must shift from fear to faith. We all must go from fearing to trusting! Remember this as well: Doubt is your enemy too. When you are operating in doubt, you're unable to trust! Only believe and know that God is good and He will see you through anything that comes your way.

Chapter

27

The Spirit of Grief
This will help you overcome.

One night while I was trying to sew, I looked up and saw Katherine's picture. In a flash, grief hit my heart, hard! I found myself on the floor. The pain became so overwhelming I couldn't lift myself up. My husband heard my cry and came running in to help, saying, "What's wrong? Baby, what's wrong?"

I was sobbing so hard that I couldn't even answer him. I just pointed to her picture. He picked me up from the floor and suggested that I go wash my face then head to bed. I did as he said. Once I crawled into bed the overwhelming pain returned. I told my husband that the pain wasn't going away and that I needed to talk to God. I then got up and went into the living room and got on my knees.

I wept. I cried out, "Lord, this is more than I can bare." He spoke to me, "Jennifer, bind grief and regret and loose my peace." The second I did as He said, I felt the pain lift off of me and His peace flooded my heart.

The next morning, I read about two deadly enemies. Their names are grief and sorrow. These two emotions are dangerous because the force behind these emotions are actually spiritual beings sent by the devil himself to kill, steal and destroy.

Understand that there is a natural grieving process, which we all must go through when we lose a loved one. As I experienced that, there is a spirit of grief that is meant to take you out. How often have you seen someone who has lost a loved one but for some reason cannot recover from it?

The evil spirit of grief is overwhelming and very destructive. If you have been overwhelmed with losing a loved one, know that you can bind the spirit of grief and loose the peace of God.

Submit yourselves, then, to God. Resist the devil, and he will flee from you. (James 4:7 NIV)

The process of binding and loosing took place the instant I spoke the words out loud, just as God instructed me. Peace flooded into my heart and the aching disappeared in seconds!

I will give you the keys of the kingdom of heaven; whatever you bind on earth will be bound in heaven, and whatever you loose on earth will be loosed in heaven." (Matthew 16:19). NIV

If you need to speak that prayer, let me help you.

Say it out loud: "I bind the spirit of grief and regret and loose the peace of God over my life. In Jesus' name."

You can do the same with sorrow. Say, "I bind sorrow and loose joy! In Jesus' name!"

Chapter

28

Knowing Your Enemy is Vital

Satan and his demons hate God and all of mankind. Satan is a mastermind of deception. His goal for mankind is to kill, steal and destroy. Satan sets you up to believe you don't need God, or that he or God aren't real, major deception.

YOU DON'T FIGHT THE CREATOR, or *YOU WILL, "FOR SURE LOSE EVERY TIME!"*

The hatred the enemy has for mankind is **NOT** a game, it's a real war. Our fight is spiritual; not against flesh and blood. Allow me to say it again, the **devil is real and he hates us with a passion**. He uses people to destroy one another, *while God partners with people to heal one another.*

The Lord sent His Holy Spirit to lead us into all truth. He lives inside of the believer. The Holy Spirit only comes when invited in. God needs us to partner with Him to restore what was stolen. You might say, "Why doesn't God just wipe the enemy out!" He will, but He wants you with Him first. Please don't waste time thinking you have time playing with disobedience. It's deadly and eternal.

The enemy needs a host to work through, so his entrance in is agreement with wickedness, disobedience and pride. He comes without permission. **He simply looks for the open door through disobedience. The open-door Adam and Eve gave the enemy was through their disobedience.**

As you may already know, life is a two-way street. Either you're serving God or the enemy. The enemy drives, Jesus draws. The enemy is a liar, Jesus is truth. The enemy destroys and deceives, Jesus loves and restores.

Who do you want to serve? If you say, "I don't want to serve anybody!" First, realize this: You are serving one or the other.

The enemy wanted to be God, he wanted God's position. It's what got him kicked out of heaven. He wanted to be greater than God, but there is only *one* who is supreme. There is only *one* true God. When the devil decided to be his own god, he got the boot! He was cast out of God's presence and became the arch enemy of God and mankind.

Don't be deceived in thinking you can be your own God. You will put yourself in the same position of the enemy.

When the first man and woman were created, they failed to trust God's command to not eat from the Tree of Knowledge of Good and Evil. They fell prey to the enemy and lost full dominion. They gave up their privileges. God literally instructed them **not** to eat from one tree throughout that beautiful paradise, and they just couldn't resist the one thing God said not to do. They were surround with beauty and lavished with everything needed.

---

16 And the Lord God commanded the man, "You are free to eat from any tree in the garden; 17 but you must not eat from the tree of the knowledge of good and evil, for when you eat from it you will certainly die." Genesis 2:9 NIV

They walked with God and were in His presence all the time. Can you imagine how amazing that must have been? They disobeyed and it cost them their life. It cost them spiritual death, to be without the spirit of God within them. It took Jesus dying on the cross to become right with God again. He is the only one who could give us back the spirit of God.

God desires for His creation to receive love, when you receive love it's easy to love back. He wants to be loved back!

By His grace, mankind has been given the free will to choose. I love free will! God is Love and love is free, it is not demanding. God's love doesn't force us to do one thing or another. It simply offers us the opportunity to love and be loved. Because of free will, we don't have to, we get to!

Get this: we have free will to walk with God every day and learn His ways. We can choose to beat the enemy daily or give into his tactics of temptation and disobedience. But when we disobey, we let the enemy beat us. The choice is ours! Do we receive God's love or the enemy's wrath and destruction? The purpose of creation is so that God could lavish His love on you and me within the context of a covenant relationship.

The Lord is love. All He can give is love! Indeed, He is righteous and just. Of course, He is an all-knowing judge. But His decisions are always rooted in love, truth, righteousness and justice. Would you rather have God made us all robotic and take away our free will?

During the years of my pain and sorrow on earth, I learned that the enemy is prowling around seeking who he will devour, just like Scripture tells us. It is up to us to fight that beast and put him in his place. So how do we fight back? We get in covenant relationship with the creator Himself.

Jesus has beaten the enemy and has given us *His* authority, stripping the enemy of his rights and privileges. The enemy only has the legal right that was given to him at the fall of man. Nothing more.

Thankfully, the Father, Son and The Holy Ghost were all together as one in the beginning of creation. It was then that there was a reconciliation plan already in place for the fall of man. When the time was right, Jesus stepped down from heaven and in all humility, became a seed in a virgin womb, was raised up as a human, showed us that we could overcome the wiles of the enemy, only with Him. Then He died in our place as the perfect sacrifice for our sins. He came to take back what was stolen in the Garden of Eden.

When Jesus died on the cross, His shed blood redeemed us from the curse that was put on Adam at the fall. The Bible says that Jesus will come back to earth to get his people. We are called the Bride of Christ. The devil is doing everything in his power to delay the return of Christ, because he knows his time is short. God will destroy the darkness off the earth, and those that are with Him will live in Glory with Him. Those that serve themselves, are actually serving the enemy' they will be destroyed with the devil.

Jesus is beckoning you to receive Him as your Savior, comforter, and God. He wants all to come to repentance and share life with Him.

Without Jesus, you receive the wrath along with the enemy because you are choosing to do so.

When you become a child of God, you get your authority back! You get the dominion back! You partner with God, not against Him. By the way, Jesus is no wimp. He's extremely powerful and all knowing. You can bet He knows who, what, when, where, and how to win in every situation.

Chapter

29

Army of the Lord

It was the summer of 2009; I was one of the camp counselors for the annual youth retreat. The retreat was held at the beach, one of my favorite places to be with God. I made sure I woke up earlier than the kids to spend a quiet time with the Lord.

As I was walking along the beach talking to God, I was enjoying the handiwork of His creation. The sun looks as if it's coming out of the water and then the array of light seems to sparkle like diamonds making it all the more spectacular. Each time I see the sun rise it always appears to come from the deep, reminding me of how wide, long, high, and deep God's love is. It's un-ending. I love the feel of the soft white sand, the rush of water flowing under my feet. I especially love the freshness of the new day.

During my walk one morning, I was talking to Jesus about being a soldier in His army, and within seconds of our conversation. I kicked up a toy soldier! A little green plastic toy soldier surfaced from the sand! What were the odds of finding a toy soldier during that conversation? I picked up the soldier in awe of what had just happened. I took the soldier into the youth meeting and gave it to the leader to use in his sermon that day. Funny how God works.

The following Tuesday was my Bible college night. It was the first day of my third year, and the school was in a different location than usual. As I walked into the door there stood a life size cardboard army man stating, "GOD CHOSE YOU!" I felt his presence all over me. **We are in army of the Lord, and we are at war, and need to be in an offensive position at all times.** *At that moment, I felt that God was saying, "front-line soldier."*

We were given a book to read, "Evangelism by Fire" written by Reinhard Bonnke, a German Pentecostal evangelist known principally for his gospel missions throughout Africa. Reinhard Bonnke has been an evangelist and missionary in Africa since 1967. He is a very amazing man and it would do you good to read many of his books. He has gotten millions of people saved. I was early to class, so I began to read the newly assigned book. As I began reading, I could feel the presence of the Lord all over me! I was new at this school and didn't know anyone in this class. I was trying to contain myself, but I couldn't do it. The teacher began to speak, but I simply couldn't repress what I was feeling, I apologized to the teacher for what I felt was interruption, and she simply stated, "That's alright, that's exactly what this school is about. It's the kind of school we are. A full gospel-spirit-filled school. The presence of God is always welcomed here." She could see that God was touching me in a powerful way.

I wasn't trying to sound dramatic, but it was powerful. As for being called into **His army, I'm all in.** I will continue to co-labor with Him so He could touch all that I come in contact with.

The little things like finding the army soldier in the sand, and then the Full Size-Army soldier as I walked through the door at the college simply confirms what he is saying to me. His power and presence can't be denied. His word equips us for the call. **We are in a spiritual war and our fight is supernatural.** The enemy uses things in the natural to distract, trick, and deceive us. We must put on our armor and know God's word, which is our sword to fight in the battle.

Deception is the enemy's plan; our battle starts with wrong thinking. The enemy plants a thought, and when we agree with the wrong thought, we get into trouble. If we begin to believe the lie, then the enemy gets a foot in the door. Learning who we are in Christ is of utmost importance. The battle is the Lord's, but we must walk in agreement with Him. Without being in agreement with the Lord, we don't stand a chance. The enemy is not playing, and neither should we. Even though we are on the winning team, many people perish for lack of knowledge.

It's imperative to get to know Jesus as your savior. If you reject getting to know the truth you put yourself and your children in grave danger. Please don't ignore when The Holy Spirit draws you to repentance. He's ready and waiting for you to get to know him.

"Because you have rejected knowledge,
I also reject you as my priests;
because you have ignored the law of your God,
I also will ignore your children." Hosea 4:6

It's up to us to get the knowledge and learn to fight. Some ask why didn't God save them from death, after all, He's God. God is saying, I've put my word and sword in your hand to fight. Cooperate with me and you win!

My Prayer for YOU

14 For this reason I kneel before the Father, 15 from whom every family in heaven and on earth derives its name. 16 I pray that out of his glorious riches he may strengthen you with power through his Spirit in your inner being, 17 so that Christ may dwell in your hearts through faith. And I pray that you, being rooted and established in love, 18 may have power, together with all the Lord's holy people, to grasp how wide and long and high and deep is the love of Christ, 19 and to know this love that surpasses knowledge—that you may be filled to the measure of all the fullness of God.

20 Now to him who is able to do immeasurably more than all we ask or imagine, according to his power that is at work within us, 21 to him be glory in the church and in Christ Jesus throughout all generations, for ever and ever! Amen. (Ephesians 3:14-21)

Chapter

30

Turn the Other Cheek

We hadn't been in Georgia long. I didn't know my way around very well and I needed to shop for a car. My three children, ages 11, 7, and 2 were with me. I was on my way to test drive a car in location I was not familiar with at all. It was the year 1989 and there were no cell phones or GPS at the time. Life wasn't as convenient as it is now.

I was lost. I had all the directions written down, but that wasn't enough. I was still lost! I was making a turn off the road when suddenly, a young lady appeared on her bike from out of nowhere and I accidentally cut her off. At that point, I decided to completely get off of the main road to get my barring's straight. I turned into a subdivision to get a good look at my notes and avoid any more loss of time or problems.

I pulled into a neighborhood and then into someone's driveway to turn around. As I was backing out of the driveway, wouldn't you know it, I cut the same girl off again! She came flying behind my car as I was backing out. "Oh my gosh, I'm so sorry!" Well, she wasn't at all happy. She jumped off her bike and **suddenly punched me in my face**! I was stunned! I went to grab the door handle, not sure of what I was going to do. Immediately I heard, "**Turn the other cheek!**" The Holy Spirit spoke so quickly! What? Tears welled up in my eyes. That upset me, I shouted out the window, "I hope Jesus blesses you the same way you blessed me!" Wow, that was just great! I fixed her, right. LOL. Every time I think of my response, I still laugh.

My children were very upset as well. I continued to pull off, but when I looked in my review mirror, I saw the girl on the ground with her hands covering her face. She was crying! I said, "Oh that's just great, I guess you want me to go minister to her, right?"

When my children heard me say that to Jesus, they all started screaming, "No, Mom!' 'She punched you in the face!' 'Mom, No!" All three of them were crying. I let them know I would be fine, and Jesus wanted me to help this lady.

I got out of the car, and picked her up off the ground. She stood up and put her head onto my shoulder and cried even more, "I'm so sorry, I don't know why I did that, I just got saved last night."

"Oh, that explains it. I know why you did that; the devil isn't happy about you getting saved. Now you're no longer his."

I forgave and prayed for her and then I left. The enemy was hot on her trail.

That evening, while washing the dishes, I was whining about what happened to Jesus. "Lord, she punched me in my face! Look at the knot on my face!" He spoke gently, "Jennifer they plucked out my beard". That changed my thoughts quickly. Wow, the thought of all that Jesus had suffered for us was overwhelming. Such horrible beatings and terrible treatment leading to His death. The fact that He didn't have to endure this, but He chose to do it for us. He took so much abuse, he was innocent. He didn't deserve any of the sorrows He went through. But He did it all for us.

Isaiah 53 MSG

Who believes what we've heard and seen?
Who would have thought God's saving power would look like this?

2-6 The servant grew up before God—a scrawny seedling,
a scrubby plant in a parched field.
There was nothing attractive about him,

nothing to cause us to take a second look.
He was looked down on and passed over,
  a man who suffered, who knew pain firsthand.
One look at him and people turned away.
  We looked down on him, thought he was scum.
But the fact is, it was our pains he carried—
  our disfigurements, all the things wrong with us.
We thought he brought it on himself,
  that God was punishing him for his own failures.
But it was our sins that did that to him,
  that ripped and tore and crushed him—our sins!
He took the punishment, and that made us whole.
  Through his bruises we get healed.
We're all like sheep who've wandered off and gotten lost.
  We've all done our own thing, gone our own way.
And God has piled all our sins, everything we've done wrong,
  on him, on him.

⁷⁻⁹ He was beaten, he was tortured,
  but he didn't say a word.
Like a lamb taken to be slaughtered
  and like a sheep being sheared,
  he took it all in silence.
Justice miscarried, and he was led off—
  and did anyone really know what was happening?
He died without a thought for his own welfare,
  beaten bloody for the sins of my people.
They buried him with the wicked,
  threw him in a grave with a rich man,
Even though he'd never hurt a soul
  or said one word that wasn't true.

¹⁰ Still, it's what God had in mind all along,
  to crush him with pain.
The plan was that he give himself as an offering for sin

so that he'd see life come from it—life, life, and more life.
    And God's plan will deeply prosper through him.

[11-12] Out of that terrible travail of soul,
    he'll see that it's worth it and be glad he did it.
Through what he experienced, my righteous one, my servant,
    will make many "righteous ones,"
    as he himself carries the burden of their sins.
Therefore I'll reward him extravagantly—
    the best of everything, the highest honors—
Because he looked death in the face and didn't flinch,
    because he embraced the company of the lowest.
He took on his own shoulders the sin of the many,
    he took up the cause of all the black sheep.

Chapter

31

Dream Again

As I look back over my life, I wholeheartedly thank God. I'm at a place in my life now where I can dream again. My fears, desires, and even my highest expectations are in His hands. My role is to purposefully stay close to His heart like a child does with a parent. *Be childlike!*

When I think about it, I absolutely love how you and I came from God's imagination. We were hand-picked and created from the very beginning of creation because He planned it. We are 100% thought of in His imagination. He designed each and every one of us. We are His masterpiece as He graciously gave us all imaginations; as well.

Adults talk about how imagination is something that only children are expected to have, but nothing could be further from the truth. Where do you think you get your dreams from? The positive dreams and imaginations that you see and feel in your heart were put there by God Himself. He has placed His specific desires in each of us.

We are created in the image of God. When we have children, they look and act like us. We too have dreams, wishes, and desires for them. It's the same way with our heavenly Father. Supernaturally, His desires are placed in the hearts of every believer to live out on Earth. I personally believe that we actually become who He designed us to be the moment we tap into His plan. Think about it. Do you ever wonder how the desire to become a doctor, lawyer, teacher, athlete, minister, etc., was placed into that mind and heart of yours? Is that not part of God's plan? We don't feel a full rest about ourselves until we are walking in what we were called to do.

The world would not operate the way it does if it were not for God's specific order and timing. This includes you being born for such a time as this. Do you think everything is just one big coincidence? Do you think that it's by chance that people all over the globe just so happen to choose what he or she will do in life? Without a plan, we are lost. We wouldn't know which way to go.

One thing I know for sure is this: God has not lost control of His creation. Humanity thinks they're in control, but no way! Read your Bible. In fact, He is in full control. We are still living out the Author's storyline. Even though some of our friends and family members didn't fulfill their calling, don't think for one moment that their lives weren't accounted for.

"For you created my inmost being; you knit me together in my mother's womb. I praise you because I am fearfully and wonderfully made; your works are wonderful; I know that full well." (Psalm 139:13-14, KJV)

"But the very hairs of your head are all numbered. Do not fear therefore; you are of more value than many sparrows." (Luke 12:7, KJV)

It's childlike faith that pleases the Father. He wants us to believe like a child. Being His child takes all the stress and anxieties away. It is well known that children laugh more than adults. They have more fun and fewer worries. It's a fact. As believers, we are not supposed to worry and be so wrapped up in every little thing that goes wrong. When something does go wrong, a child doesn't dwell on it for too long. They simply move on. A child's problems are placed in their parents' hands with an assurance that they've got it. Oh, how I wish we adults could let go of things more easily, and that's exactly what God wants from us too. Jesus said, "children are the greatest in His Kingdom." He wants us to become childlike, even as adults.

Yet it begins with us being born again. Once we do that, we'll have so much more to laugh about.

Have you noticed that children are so close to the spirit of God? It's when the so called "grown-ups" feed children their thoughts that they began to believe with a clouded view.

"Don't be silly, it's only your imagination, adults say." A child, because of their purity, can see and hear God more clearly. It's when information gets filtered through the believe of the adults that it becomes distorted.

God always delivers from a place of love. People deliver from knowledge or fear. Whose knowledge is it? Is it the knowledge that's has been passed down from one generation to the next? Filtered through unbelief or ridicule.

We know that knowledge puffs up, but love builds up. If we would go to the source of Love, we will find the childlike faith. We then are open to receive the revelation of who God is. Then you will see Him as a loving, caring father who wants what's best for us. Give your knowledge to God, and receive His counsel. When you do, you realize He is LOVE.

—— The Greatest in the Kingdom of Heaven ——

At one point in history, the disciples came to Jesus and asked the question, "Who, then, is the greatest in the kingdom of heaven?" Jesus called a little child to Him and placed the child among them. Now, observe the words of the Lord.

He said, "Truly I tell you, unless you change and become like little children, you will never enter the kingdom of heaven. Therefore, whoever takes the lowly position of this child is the greatest in the kingdom of heaven. And whoever welcomes one such child in my name welcomes me (Matthew 18:1-4 KJV).

I understand that many men and women missed out on a healthy relationship with their earthly father, but I know this much, man cannot give us what only God can. Our need for a true and unconditional love is something that can only come from a relationship with God.

Now don't get me wrong. I'm not saying you don't need people in your life to play a motherly or fatherly role. Like God, fellowship and intimacy with others is very important. What I'm saying is that, only God can fill your heart's desires. You cannot experience true love without God being involved. Everything you've experienced up to this point might've merely been a worldly love. However, I would be doing you a disservice if I didn't promote the greatest love of all – the one that Jesus tells us about throughout the Gospels.

If you don't know Jesus, allow me to introduce you to Him. His Spirit is ever-present and very much alive. He is ready to heal you and pardon you of your past sins and your past hurts. He covers your sins with His Blood and the darkness flees. When His light comes into your heart, you will feel lighter, cleaner, and more alive. The closer you get to God, the more you learn to love yourself and others. I can truly say that He restores life! The prayer is so simple. Just invite Him into your heart today by saying these words and believing them with faith:

Heavenly Father, I come to you in the name of Your Son, Jesus. I repent of my sins. Your Word says, if I confess with my mouth that Jesus is Lord and believe in my heart that God raised Him from the dead, then I will be saved. For it is with my heart that I believe and am justified. And it is with my mouth that I confess and am saved. The Bible tells me that anyone who trusts in You will never be put to shame.

It says that everyone who calls on Your name, Lord, shall be saved. I choose you, Jesus. Come fill me with Your presence. Clean my heart of sin and pain. Thank You for filling me with Your Holy Spirit and make me new. Amen

---

If you read those words and have asked Jesus to live in your heart, you are saved! Proclaim Him as your Lord and Savior. Read your Bible as often as possible and surround yourself with other born-again believers. If you read the prayer and meant it, then you've officially received your *Spirit Eyes*!

Printed in the United States
By Bookmasters